TO BE A U.S. NAVAL AVIATOR

JAY A. STOUT

ZENITH PRESS

First published in 2005 by Zenith Press, an imprint of MBI Publishing Company, Galtier Plaza, Suite 200, 380 Jackson Street, St. Paul, MN 55101-3885 USA

ISBN-13: 978-0-7603-2163-8
ISBN-10: 0-7603-2163-9

Editor: Steve Gansen
Designers: Lynn Dragonnette and LeAnn Kuhlmann

Printed in China

On the frontispiece: A view of the rear cockpit's instrument panel during an actual flight.

On the title page: A T-45 instructor's view from the rear cockpit.

On the table of contents: An LSO pays keen attention as his student approaches the ramp of the aircraft carrier.

On the back cover:
Top: With the arresting hook down and the flaps, landing gear, and speedbrakes extended, this student is only seconds away from touching down.
Bottom: An F/A-18E Super Hornet assigned to the "Eagles" of Strike Fighter Squadron One One Five (VFA-115) launches from one of four steam-powered catapults aboard the Nimitz-class aircraft carrier *USS John C. Stennis* (CVN 74). *USN/Mark J. Rebilas*

On the cover: The constricted confines of the cockpit. The tangle of straps and buckles that makes up the pilot's flight gear is apparent. *USMC/John Andress*

About the Author

Jay Stout was born in Indianapolis, Indiana in 1959. After graduating from Purdue University in 1981 he was commissioned into the Marine Corps. Subsequent to being designated a naval aviator in 1983, he flew the F-4 Phantom and the F/A-18 Hornet and flew 37 combat missions during Operation DESERT STORM. He retired in

2001 after accumulating nearly 4,800 flight hours. Following his retirement he worked for a major airline for several months but was furloughed after the terrorist attacks of September 11, 2001. After a year flying F/A-18s for the Kuwait Air Force as a pilot instructor he returned to the States and now works in the defense industry. Aside from *To Be a U.S. Naval Aviator*, another of his works will also be released during 2005. *Hammer from Above: Marine Aviation Over Iraq* details the role of Marine Corps aviation during the 2003 campaign to topple Saddam Hussein. Stout lives in San Diego with his wife and two daughters.

CONTENTS

Acknowledgments

The clean lines of the T-45 are evident here. It looks like a combat jet.

When I initially signed up for this project I thought that it would be a big, fat softball—something I could do in my spare time with my eyes closed. After all, I had gone through the training a couple of decades earlier and had been a flight instructor later in my career. What could be so difficult about putting together a few thousand words and a couple of hundred photographs?

Well, as I soon learned, there is a lot more to tell beyond what my matriculation and skills as a fighter pilot encompassed. For instance, I had no experience with rotary wing training or operations. Sure, I could distinguish a helicopter from a jet three times out of five, but I knew next to nothing about the associated training pipeline. The same was true about the multi-engine syllabus. Too, I needed to be careful not to make assumptions about primary training and the jet pipeline just because it was the route I had traveled; a lot of things have changed since the 1980s.

Fortunately there were plenty of folks ready to help. To say that the U.S. Navy was ready to drop everything just to help a little-known writer would be an overstatement. I definitely had to do a bit of whining, wheedling, and cajoling. Still, enough Navy professionals stepped forward so that I was able to make this book as good as it is. Lieutenant Matt Galan, deputy director, Navy Office of Information East, was very helpful and more than ready to throw his weight around to help when required. Lieutenant Rob Lyon, the Public Affairs Officer for CNATRA, led me around NAS Corpus Christi and put me in touch with many of the different offices I needed to contact. Ms. Sheri Crowe at NAS Pensacola put together a fantastic tour of the training efforts there and was very helpful with my requests for follow-up information. The staff at the Naval Aerospace Medical Institute was first-rate in their willingness to answer questions. Mr. Andrew Thomas squired me around NAS Kingsville and Mr. Paul Nelson did the same at NAS Whiting Field. Mr. Mike Maus worked hard to get me out to the aircraft carrier during student qualifications. First Lieutenant Victoria Jennings took me around my old stomping grounds at MCAS Miramar, and

Cruise formation is different from parade formation. It allows the flight lead to maneuver more aggressively without worrying about a wingman running into him.

Lieutenant Colonel Rich "Big Bird" Westmoreland greased the skids to get me into Major "Clyde" Wingard's cockpit for a T-45 training sortie. Others who provided invaluable help were Captain Thomas Hills, Colonel Mike "Gumby" Sawyers, Lieutenant Colonel Ronald "Pee Wee" Colyer, Major Tom "Vito" Carnesi, Second Lieutenant Nicole Poff (USAF), Captain John "Doogie" Andress, Captain Fred "Chewy" Pierce, Major Edward "2-Dog" Vicknair and Ms. Lori Aprilliano.

I can't say enough good things about the image archives the Navy and Marine Corps make available online. The photographs are easy to find, numerous, and of very good quality. These two services are to be commended for the excellence of their photography specialists. Please note their names in the captions; if there is no photographer noted, this indicates that I shot the image. I am self-trained and consider myself adequate with a camera, but my task was made much easier by the excellent Lumix FZ20 digital camera by Panasonic. It's easy to use and the outstanding

12X optical lens is a lifesaver. Its high pixel count also provides a great deal of versatility. Just for the record, I don't own any Panasonic stock, I bought the camera at retail and my name means nothing to them.

The best part about writing this book was visiting with the students. Rest assured that they are more than capable of winning this nation's wars and are imbued with the same fine qualities that have distinguished naval aviators since the early part of the last century. I'm extremely jealous of the careers they have in front of them and would gladly divorce my wife, disavow my children and sell my house in order to trade places.

Well, perhaps I wouldn't sell my house.

All kidding aside, my wife and daughters have been very supportive of my work. I love them very much.

Finally, many thanks to Eric Hammel, the great World War II aviation writer, for pointing this project my way, to my agent, E.J. McCarthy, and to Steve Gansen and the fine staff at MBI Publishing Company/Zenith Press.

ONE

The ultimate goal, the naval aviator's Wings of Gold. These are the wings worn by naval aviators regardless of the types of aircraft they are assigned to fly. The design has changed little since the first devices were issued in 1918.

Routes to Training

The "shooter" has given his signal. An instant later, this student will be hurtling airborne.

There likely is not a male in the United States beyond the age of ten who has not at one time or another imagined himself behind the controls of a U.S. Navy jet—rocketing off the bow of an aircraft carrier or twisting through the sky in deadly aerial duels with enemy aircraft. It is the stuff of *Top Gun*. But increasingly it is not just males who are caught up in the dream of flying in our nation's sea service; more and more women aspire to the same goal. And naval aviation is not just jets and aircraft carriers; it is helicopters and big, multi-engine patrol aircraft, as well as the men and women who maintain and support them. Likewise, naval aviation is not just made up of the U.S. Navy; the Marine Corps air element—one of the biggest air forces in the world in its own right—is pure naval aviation. Marine crews are trained by the U.S. Navy and operate side by side with their sea-service brothers through their entire careers. And the U.S. Coast Guard should not be forgotten. Although the roles that Coast Guard fliers play are often quite distinct from those of their Navy brothers, they are trained and regulated by the same rules as that service. And like the Corps, the U.S. Coast Guard's heritage is closely intertwined with that of the larger service.

Tom Cruise aside, the F-14 Tomcat was the real star of the 1986 movie *Top Gun*. USN/Daniel McLain

But how does one become a naval aviator? What path do young men or women who truly want to fly for the U.S. Navy follow? Must they be superhuman? Do they have to possess the academic acumen of a Harvard PhD candidate and the physical prowess of an Olympic athlete? As is true with most of the best things in life, what the young person who strives to be a naval aviator needs most is persistence and the willingness to do what it takes to reach a goal. Certainly there are basic requirements. Foremost is a college

degree backed by a transcript that shows at least average grades or better. And while it cannot hurt to have the physical attributes of a world-class athlete, this is hardly a prerequisite; most healthy young adults stand a very real chance of meeting the U.S. Navy's physical standards.

Among the great multitudes that speculate about a career in naval aviation, the percentage that actually follows through and investigates the different routes that lead toward earning the coveted Wings of Gold is tiny. This

The U.S. Navy operates more than 750 training aircraft, including nearly 200 T-45s.

is a natural part of the selection process. The training required to become a naval aviator demands initiative and commitment. Those who demonstrate only a passing interest and who do not have the energy and resourcefulness to pursue that interest are probably not good candidates for the years of training required to make a combat aviator. Those who do investigate the different means by which they can enter naval aviator training will find that there are several different paths; these will be discussed later in this chapter.

The young men and women who want to pursue a career as Navy, Marine Corps, or Coast Guard pilots must complete special testing to ascertain their suitability and aptitude for aviation training. Each service tests uniquely, and each assigns its candidates to aviation billets differently. For example, the Marine Corps is currently the only branch of the armed forces that offers a guarantee for flight training before candidates even receive a college diploma. Of course, this is contingent on the aspirants' actually earning a degree and then successfully completing all the required examinations. The Navy offers guarantees

from time to time, depending on its needs, as does the U.S. Coast Guard. Because policies change so often, it is important that interested persons contact their recruiters to get the latest information.

The single test for selection to flight training used universally by all three services is the Aviation Selection Test Battery, or ASTB. Of all the young men and women in the United States who ever dream of becoming naval pilots, only about 10,000 actually take this set of exams each year. The test has its roots in World War II, and although it has gone through several revisions in the six-plus decades since its inception, it remains largely unchanged—mostly because it has been such an accurate predictor of whether or not an individual will succeed or fail.

The ASTB is actually made up of five timed subtests: mathematics and verbal (MVT), mechanical comprehension (MCT), aviation and nautical (ANT), spatial apperception (SAT), and an aviation interest (AI) survey. These are all multiple-choice tests and are similar in format to most standardized examinations. The MVT evaluates basic math aptitude and writing comprehension. The MCT tests a

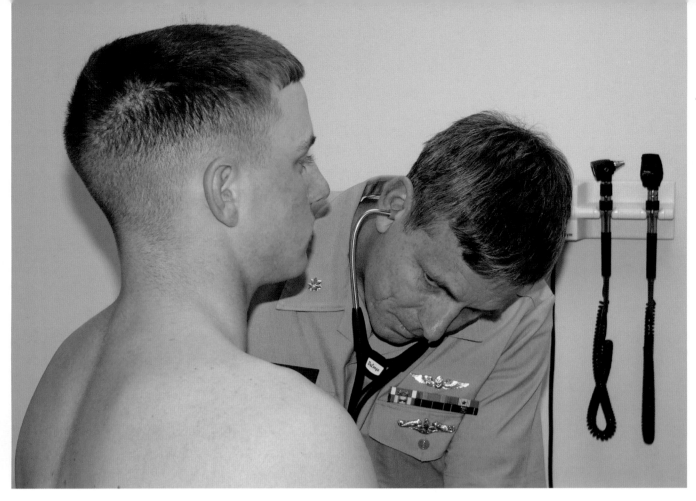

Although the examination is thorough, most young, healthy adults stand a reasonably good chance of being declared fit for flight status.

The ability to read a chart is no guarantee that a would-be aviator's eyes will be good enough for the U.S. Navy.

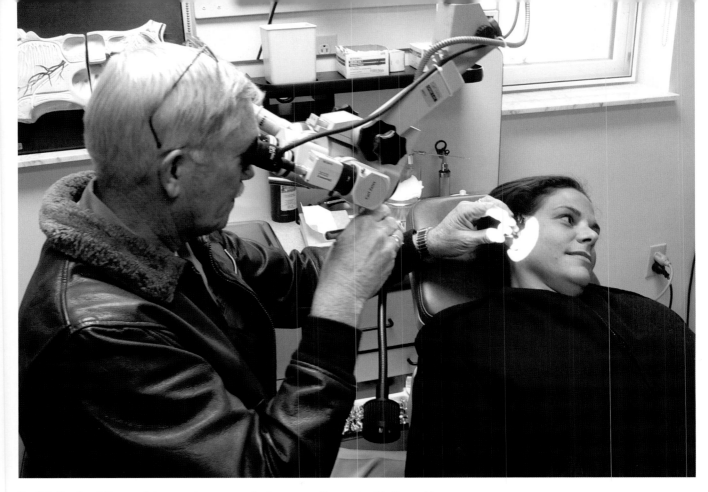

The U.S. Navy's aviation medicine experts are recognized as among the very best in the world.

candidate's knowledge of simple mechanics and physics. Perhaps the most challenging is the SAT: it challenges the individual's situational and spatial awareness by presenting photographs of different types of terrain as viewed from a cockpit. The candidate must match the picture against a set of aircraft that are positioned in different attitudes. Finally, the ANT evaluates a person's aviation and nautical knowledge. The tests are now given on line, and the entire test battery can be taken in less than three hours. Results are available immediately after completion.

In addition to the different physical and educational requirements noted, entry to service academies or Officer Candidate School (OCS) courses also depends on other factors. Prospective officers cannot have been convicted of a felony, for instance (and there are some years when the competition is so stiff that even a handful of speeding tickets will disqualify an applicant). A history of drug abuse will eliminate any chance of success. Age can also rule out a commission; strictures on age differ from service to service, and sometimes there are differences in programs within the individual services. Generally, officer candidates should strive to be commissioned no later than their

twenty-seventh or twenty-eighth birthday, although sometimes waivers can be granted even beyond thirty years.

Requirements change frequently in all the branches of the armed forces, and it cannot be emphasized enough that the latest, most up-to-date information resides with the officer recruiter. A visit to the recruiter's office is the first step that a would-be naval aviator must take.

There is a widespread perception that the average naval aviator is a model-perfect physical specimen—someone with the strength and guts to complete back-to-back triathlons. Although naval aviation counts many serious athletes among its ranks, including Olympic competitors, the physical requirements are not out of the reach of many young adults. Certainly most university students of modest athletic ability and normal height and weight have a good chance at passing the required medical screenings.

"I wanted to be a pilot, but my eyes weren't good enough." This is perhaps the single most frequent phrase that naval aviators hear from a stranger who learns that they fly in the military. In the past, the requirement for perfect, 20/20 vision was seldom waived and was the most common reason that aspiring young men were turned away from service as pilot candidates. Things have

The naval aviator must be in outstanding physical condition and possess good stamina. Operations in Iraq during 2003 saw some crews in the cockpits for nearly 20 hours. *USMC/Jose Ponce*

changed for the would-be aviator with less than flawless eyesight. Currently, candidates with vision as poor as 20/40 are considered physically qualified so long as corrective lenses can improve their eyesight to 20/20. And whereas photorefractive keratectomy (PRK) surgery was previously an automatic disqualifier, medical waivers for this procedure are now quite often granted. On the other hand, laser-assisted in-situ keratomileusis (popularly known as LASIK), a different sort of eye surgery, is not waivable and there is no current plan to make it so.

What this relatively recent change in policy does is broaden the pool of prospective aviators, thereby giving the U.S. Navy the opportunity to be more selective in areas other than eyesight. Of course, regulations can and do change, and interested persons must check with their recruiter for the latest regulations.

Just as the standards for eyesight have become more flexible, the U.S. Navy's Operational Medicine Institute has been able to clear candidates for flight duty who might have been denied only a decade or so earlier. This increased flexibility has been made possible by advances in medical

The U.S. Marines are not the only ones who get physical. These "plebes" from the U.S. Naval Academy build teamwork while they build their physiques. *USN/Brien Aho*

The U.S. Naval Academy admits approximately 1,200 young men and women each year. *USN/Dana Howe*

technology and training. In the past, the Navy denied flight status to individuals for a malady or condition simply to be on the safe side, but new procedures, technologies, and equipment allow the service's aerospace medicine experts to investigate an apparently disqualifying condition more thoroughly to determine its possible effects in the cockpit. In many cases, candidates with a condition that previously would have eliminated them from training will be allowed to continue.

Every case is different, and it is difficult to predict the final outcome. There is also a justifiable tendency to "save" fliers already in training instead of potential candidates who have yet to start. The U.S. Navy is more anxious to protect investments it has already made: budgets are perpetually tight, and the service is accountable for what it spends. But any young man or woman in reasonably good health and free of chronic medical disorders should feel little anxiety about fitness for service as a naval aviator.

Typically, after applicants have successfully completed the batteries of aptitude and suitability tests, they are scheduled for an initial flight physical examination at a regional U.S. Navy facility with the necessary equipment and personnel. The exam lasts the better part of a day and

is likely the most comprehensive physical assessment that the candidates have ever undergone. The examination commences with the applicants completing an in-depth health history that gives the Navy's professionals a good idea of the individuals' medical background. Anthropometric measurements are taken to ensure individuals will be able to fit into a cockpit. This is not only to make certain that they can manipulate the controls, but to ensure that they will not be at undue risk of injury in the event of an ejection. Vision, as discussed before, is also tested. Visual acuity is extremely important, and good depth perception is also required; color blindness usually precludes service as an aviator. Of course, the eyes must be free of any disease or abnormalities.

Hearing is tested for obvious reasons, and the ears, nose, and throat undergo close scrutiny. The ears are especially sensitive and play an important role in maintaining balance; a malformed or diseased ear canal can cause debilitating sickness and disorientation, or even pain, while individuals are airborne. Blood and urine samples are drawn because these can give valuable clues about an applicants' health that might otherwise not be apparent. A set of X-rays is taken, and an exhaustive battery of

During the four years the midshipmen are at the academy, Bancroft Hall serves as their home. *USN/Damon Moritz*

cardiovascular tests is conducted as well as a dental exam. Finally, all are examined as complete individuals for any defects that might ultimately render them physically unqualified or aeronautically unsuitable.

The U.S. Navy has perhaps the most qualified aeromedicine experts in the world. It is impossible to quantify the lives, careers, and equipment they have saved, but their contributions to the science and service have been invaluable. Pilots quickly develop an abiding respect for their expertise, and learn to rely on "the flight docs" to address every aspect of their health.

Those who are serious about pursuing a life as a naval aviator will discover that there are several different paths that can start them toward this goal. The route that perhaps comes most commonly to mind is the U.S. Naval Academy (USNA) at Annapolis, Maryland. This is without a doubt the most rigorous way to enter Navy flight training. It is a world-renowned academic and military institution with a reputation for producing top-notch military officers. Entry into the academy is very competitive, and successful applicants must have stellar academic records, a history of leadership and achievement, and very often an impressive

The Marine Corps drill sergeants are perhaps the greatest defining influence on the U.S. Navy's officer candidates, especially during their first few weeks.

U.S. Navy OCS students go everywhere in formation.

U.S. Navy officer candidates are not often exercised in their khaki uniforms, but it will happen if their drill sergeant feels that they might benefit from an impromptu session of physical training.

The Marine Corps is the most physical of all the military services, and its trainees spend more time in the field than those of any other branch. *USMC*

varsity sports background. Typically the academy offers admission to approximately 10 percent of applicants (a recent class numbered just under 1,300).

Traditionally, those graduates from the academy that are physically qualified for service as naval aviators will receive orders to NAS Pensacola, Florida, for flight training. Of a recent graduating class made up of approximately 1,000 midshipmen, 240 men and 27 women chose to pursue a career as naval aviators. A further 60 men and 4 women elected the same careers in the Marine Corps.

The Corps does not have a separate service academy, but a significant percentage of midshipmen from the Naval Academy (about 15 percent) opt for a commission in this service. The U.S. Coast Guard has its own academy in New London, Connecticut. The missions of the U.S. Navy and Coast Guard are different although the U.S. Coast Guard Academy (USCGA), like the USNA, seeks to develop leaders for service at sea. As a result, the curriculums and styles of training and discipline are much the same. Just like their Navy counterparts, Coast Guard midshipmen take part in summer training, which includes service aboard the U.S. Coast Guard's big sailing ship, the USS

Eagle. There they learn the basics of seamanship and develop a healthy respect for the ways of the sea while acquiring confidence in their abilities to perform while afloat. As with the other service academies, the competition for entry to the USCGA is keen: the academy admits approximately 15 percent of those who apply. Its graduating classes are only about a quarter the size of those of the USNA classes, so the numbers of officers who go on to flight training are smaller. Those who perform well can expect to receive orders to flight training if they meet the various physical requirements.

Aside from the USNA, pilot-training candidates come from the Navy Reserve Officer Training Course (NROTC) or from an Officer Candidate School (OCS). These programs provide classes and training to produce officers capable of taking leadership positions at sea. The NROTC midshipmen attend military classes and drills in addition to their normal college curriculum. During the summers they report for midshipman cruises, just like their counterparts at the USNA. Scholarships are available, and monthly stipends are provided to those students who perform well enough to earn them. Like their service

The Marine Corps OCS entities are the only ones that issue weapons to the candidates. *USMC*

academy colleagues, NROTC graduates will be commissioned as ensigns in the U.S. Navy or second lieutenants in the Marine Corps upon receiving their degrees.

The U.S. Navy, Marine Corps, and Coast Guard have their own OCS. These exist not only to fill officer recruitment goals that cannot be met by the academies and ROTC programs, but also to introduce an element of diversity into the officer cadre. The outlook and approach to a problem taken by a young officer that has had only a few months of OCS training instead of that of an academy graduate may likely be different—and in some instances better. This is due in part to the OCS graduate's maturity and experience in the outside world, possibly with a number of years in civilian employment. This perspective and experience can be valuable in the military world.

In years past the U.S. Navy operated a separate OCS for its aviation program, but budget cuts and efficiency goals have driven it to combine its schools into a single thirteen-week program at NAS Pensacola.

There really is no good way to compare the curriculum of the U.S. Navy OCS with the experience provided at the USNA. OCS is essentially a crash course in military studies and conditioning for those who already have a bachelor's degree. It is intended to teach the military aspects of the naval service without the attendant core academics that are taught at the USNA, and is often described as boot camp with an emphasis on leadership. Everything is introduced at a fast and furious pace—if nothing else, the graduate of OCS will complete the course with an appreciation of time-management skills. The first week is largely consumed by in-processing activities; some of these include a review of the U.S. Navy's expectations and the introduction of basic rules and regulations. Basic drill is introduced, uniforms and books are issued, physical and mental fitness is evaluated, and haircuts are given.

While the newly commissioned officers of the U.S. Navy and Coast Guard go straight to Pensacola for flight training, the U.S. Marines train their officers for nearly six more months. *USMC*

The pace is hectic and harried by design. The candidates are rushed, bullied, and harangued to see how they act under pressure. They are given tasks that are impossible to accomplish in the time allotted and are disciplined for failing to complete them. There is a lot of yelling by the instructors. (Nearly every candidate has second thoughts: "I thought I woke up in hell, but realized I was in OCS.") Those who do not have the motivation or desire, or who are obviously unfit for service, are gone by the end of the first week.

Two young U.S. Marine studs try to take each other out. *USMC*

By the second week, the candidates are in their permanent living quarters and wearing standard-issue uniforms, and are being taught how to wear and keep them in accordance with regulations. Physical conditioning is begun in earnest during the first few weeks; this includes a great deal of swimming—for obvious reasons.

Also introduced early in OCS are basic engineering courses that review the rudimentary aspects of various naval propulsion systems—steam and gas turbines, diesels and aircraft engines, and nuclear power plants. Basic military customs and courtesies are taught as well as naval history and heritage. Every day also includes a great deal of organized calisthenics and impromptu physical training that can be administered as various instructors see fit.

These instructors consist of officers and senior enlisted personnel with fleet experience. But each class's most important influence—particularly early in the curriculum—is their assigned Marine Corps drill sergeant. Initially these Marines seem to be just barely removed from the devil incarnate. They strike fear into the average candidate's heart; they know and see everything, and seem to have a sixth sense that can cut straight through to shortcomings.

Typical of everything that the candidate officers do is the structure and regimentation of mealtime. It is a hurried procedure that has them moving in lockstep and eating their meals only after completing a memorized series of commands and movements. There is no talking allowed, and food, drink and utensils must be situated perfectly. Woe to the candidate who cannot conform flawlessly.

The thirteen weeks of training seem like forty-five. The middle stages of Navy OCS continue with physical training early each morning and the introduction of courses that are increasingly central to the U.S. Navy. Military law is introduced as well as administrative procedures unique to the Navy. Throughout, teamwork is stressed. If an individual has difficulties then the class has difficulties, and the class as a whole suffers the consequences when a single person fails to meet standards. This is to teach leadership and responsibility, and to develop the ability to recognize when one needs to ask for help or offer it. The best classes quickly discover that their lives are made easier when they work together rather than as individuals or as small groups.

By the time the course is half over, the typical class is given limited liberty off base during the weekends. This

Naval Flight Officers

NFOs are flying officers who are not pilots. They staff positions in U.S. Navy and Marine aircraft that require flying expertise but do not involve actual control of the aircraft. For instance, the two-seat F/A-18D Hornet, and the two-seat F/A-18F Super Hornet are crewed by pilots and NFOs who are rated as weapons system officers (WSOs). The WSOs help in the navigation of the aircraft as well as operation of the sensors, and so they also matriculate through API.

Confused yet? Wait, there's more. The backseaters in the F-14 are NFOs designated as radar intercept officers (RIOs). And the three nonpilot positions in the EA-6B are manned by NFOs who are rated as electronic countermeasures officers (ECMOs). The P-3C and EP-3E have NFOs in the crew, as does the E-6 (which is not to be confused with the EA-6B) and the E-2C.

Regardless of the NFOs not being rated pilots, the skills they bring into the cockpit are invaluable; the aircraft they crew would be less effective without them. (The gold wings of the NFO are distinguished by two anchors rather than one.)

This NFO is checking the radar aboard an S-3 Viking, prior to launching from an aircraft carrier. *USN/Michael Pusnik*

U.S. Coast Guard officer candidates develop basic seamanship skills while sailing aboard the *Eagle*. *USCG/Matthew Belson*

21

Introductory Flight Screening

Despite the academic, medical, and psychological screening that was traditionally done in the past, there were still students who had to leave flight training because they lacked the motivation, determination, or ability to adapt to an aviation environment. Many of the students dropped out of the training at their own request. Aside from the obvious inefficiencies created, the loss of these students was expensive; the failed students took training opportunities that could have been awarded to others who may have been more successful.

To decrease the attrition rate, the chief of naval air training (CNATRA, pronounced just like Frank's family name) initiated the Introductory Flight Screening program (IFS) in 2001. Under CNATRA's funding and oversight, midshipmen or officers already commissioned who are slated for training as naval aviators are required to receive twenty-five hours of instruction at an FAR Part 141–certified flight school. By the time they have received seventeen hours of dual instruction they must solo and complete at least three solo flights, one of which has to be a cross-country flight. IFS must be completed before starting API.

Civilian instructors teach the prospective naval aviators in general-aviation aircraft commonly used for training in nonmilitary flying schools. The curriculum identifies early on students who have an obvious lack of aerial aptitude. It also helps students make their own decisions about whether they have the desire or skills to pursue a career in naval aviation. The program appears to be working, and the cost appears to be more than offset by reduced attrition. It is likely that the U.S. Navy will continue IFS for at least the near term.

The basics of nautical navigation apply to naval aviation as well. Here, a U.S. Coast Guard officer candidate practices her skills from the deck of the *Eagle*. *USCG*

gives students an opportunity to spend the pay they have been collecting.

But classroom instruction continues and seamanship and navigation are introduced. The candidates do more swimming and continue their physical training with the obstacle course and longer runs. But the training gets less difficult as it continues. Drill instructors and the rest of the staff skillfully adjust their roles, becoming less domineering and threatening and more like mentors. In just a few weeks the candidates will become officers and superior in rank to the same instructors who are running their lives. The candidates will have only a short time to adjust to the new relationship.

The Marine Corps offers a few different OCS options. Unlike Navy OCS, Marine officer candidates can undergo training while they are still in college in Platoon Leaders Class, or PLC. There are two basic PLC options: The candidates can attend two six-week courses during two separate summers following their freshman year, or can attend a single ten-week course between their junior and senior years. Those who opt for training after earning their degree attend a ten-week summer course called Officer Candidates Class, or OCC. The curriculums are all essentially the same, and fall under the mantle of Marine Corps OCS. All the courses are at Quantico, Virginia.

If Navy OCS is rough, the various Marine Corps classes are nothing short of terrifying—at least initially. The moment the candidates step off the bus they are set upon by bellowing, arm-waving noncommissioned officers. Immediately their personal belongings are flung aside, and they are formed into platoons and marched through different processing stations. There is not a candidate who does not want to flee immediately—yet most of them realize that the ultimate reward will be greater than the price they will pay over the following weeks.

The next few days are spent rushing about and drawing gear, filling out paperwork, and generally preparing for the rest of the course. It all goes at a blistering pace, and at the end of the day the candidates fall asleep quickly despite the heat and humidity of the Virginia summer.

Unlike Navy OCS, where three or four candidates are quartered in individual rooms, the Corps' candidates are billeted in one large squad bay. Everyone can be seen and observed by everyone else—and by their platoon gunnery sergeant and platoon sergeant instructor. These two will be the harshest, most effective teachers the candidates will ever have. The training must be intensive; the instructors not only have to turn the candidates into Marines, but they have to make them leaders, and in less than three months!

Chief of Naval Air Training

CNATRA is charged with training all naval aviators, naval flight officers, and enlisted air crew members for not only the U.S. Navy but for the Marine Corps, and U.S. Coast Guard. The command also provides training to selected U.S. Air Force officers and officers from other nations. Headquartered at NAS Corpus Christi, Texas, CNATRA oversees the Naval Air Training Command, or NATRACOM, which is made up of five training air wings that together comprise sixteen different squadrons that operate more than 750 aircraft. These units combined fly in excess of 400,000 hours each year. NATRACOM has the responsibility for producing pilots, or naval aviators, as well as naval flight officers (NFOs). The yearly "production" of pilots varies but recently has ranged from 800 to 1,200 per year.

Matching the pilot training rate with the needs of the different services involves some amount of science, a good crystal ball, and no small bit of voodoo. Since the time for a prospective aviator to reach the fleet may be three years or more, there are a number of factors that can change the needs of the fleet, and thus the number of pilots required. The greatest of these considerations are the national economy, the elimination or introduction of different aircraft types, and the operations tempo, which in turn is driven by different armed emergencies or conflicts. None of these factors is easily predicted or controlled. The U.S. Navy and Marines both have increased the service obligations for their fliers, but this has made the task of projecting pilot training requirements only somewhat less difficult.

General-aviation aircraft like this Cessna 172 are used for introductory flight screening. *USMC/Nicholas Tremblay*

Physical training is paramount to Marine Corps officer candidates. Once commissioned, they must be able to do anything they ask of their own Marines—and more. More than the members of any other officer candidate program, prospective Marine officers must be in outstanding physical shape before they arrive for training. Calisthenics are practiced every day and runs through hills and trails are frequent. Hikes in full gear become a staple as well because they build stamina and teach the candidates how to stuff and carry their packs and weapons. Such courses include elaborate obstacles over several miles including "The Quigley," a stinking cesspool of a trench that requires candidates to totally immerse themselves in filth and goo while negotiating barbed wire and other hazards.

All Marine fliers are Marines first. When asked about their occupations, Marine officers should state that they are Marines, and then go on to explain their individual specialties (e.g., artillery or aviation). All candidates are first drilled in the basics that later are turned into infantry skills. After instruction on leadership and field skills, they are put into the field; it is in the woods and the brush, the wet and the mud, that they put the academic instruction to real use.

Teamwork is stressed, but it is the individual who is under constant evaluation. At enlisted boot camp the drill instructors are determined to get a class of young Marines trained and out to the fleet, but the candidates at OCS are scrutinized as individuals. Each must be

The CNATRA headquarters building has been in service since the early days of World War II. *USN*

capable of leading the young enlisted Marines that boot camp produces. And it is not just the training staff that does the evaluating; all the candidates are assessed on paper by each other. This gives the instructors a unique perspective that they would otherwise not have.

Close-order drill with their assigned M16 rifles is constant, and candidates become intimately familiar with their weapon.

Would-be officers are put through special confidence courses as well. These help the candidates build self-assurance on intimidating, oversized obstacles that often take teamwork to negotiate. Tactical leadership tests are also executed in the field. Individuals are put in charge of teams of varying size and evaluated on how they lead and motivate the teams to solve various problems.

Marine officer candidates stand many inspections with their uniforms, combat equipment, and rifles. They may come out of the field late in the afternoon filthy and dirty and covered with ticks and still undergo inspection the following day. Naturally, the first few inspections are not perfect, and the instructors make a great show of blustering and raging, tearing the squad bay apart.

As in any other similar course, things get better at Marine OCS as time goes on. The instructors no longer have to scare away the weaklings and instead can concentrate more on educating and developing their remaining candidates. When graduation day arrives, the graduates have been tested and proven.

Regardless of how its new officers have been commissioned, the Marine Corps does not turn them loose into the fleet until they complete six more months of training at The Basic School, or TBS. Also located at Quantico, TBS is a course that finishes the young officers before they go on to their own specialties, including pilot training. At OCS the candidates might have been exposed to certain weaponry or tactics for two or three days, at TBS the new lieutenants will spend two or three weeks on the same topic.

The different paths described are currently the only ones that lead to training the thousand or so new naval aviators produced every year. None of the schools or programs, however, is oriented only to producing pilots. The emphasis is still on training officers: all the services rightly believe that their pilots must be leaders first, and specialists second.

TWO

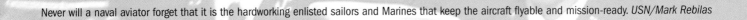

Never will a naval aviator forget that it is the hardworking enlisted sailors and Marines that keep the aircraft flyable and mission-ready. *USN/Mark Rebilas*

Aviation Preflight Indoctrination

Like many modern aircraft the T-45 has stabilators on the empennage rather than a combination of horizontal stabilizers and elevators.

Aviation preflight indoctrination (API) at NAS Pensacola is where all the prospective naval aviators finally come together. Graduates from the naval and Coast Guard academies join those who have earned their commissions through ROTC and the various OCS courses. The Marines, too, have completed their additional six months of TBS training at Quantico. For all of them, the experience is new and exciting: API is the very first course that is completely about aviation. It is made up of young officers who have a common career goal: naval aviator.

The course lasts six-and-a-half weeks. All the students are officers now and are qualified to undergo flight training. They receive introductory courses in aerodynamics, flight physiology, aircraft engines and systems, aviation weather, navigation, and flight rules and regulations. The classes are taught primarily by Navy and Marine officers in an atmosphere that is as collegiate as it is military. Although the material is comprehensive and thorough, the classes are not very difficult; the structured manner in which the material is presented is effective and the students typically do very well. Passing

Although the Super Hornet doesn't fly as fast or high as the earlier Hornet, it carries more payloads a longer distance. *USN/Daniel McLain*

requires a minimum score of 80 percent, but most achieve grades of 90 percent or better.

The aerodynamics module is made up of twelve class periods. A mix of physics and engineering, it gives the students a good grounding in the basics of flight theory. Still, some of the principles are at a level of detail that is well beyond what the young officers will use daily once they begin flying. For instance, the following learning objective is probably something the average naval aviator will never address once he leaves API: "Define the relationship between airflow velocity and cross-sectional area within a stream tube using the continuity equation." Even after a naval aviation career of more than twenty years, this author would not recognize a stream tube if it were jammed into his eye.

But a good deal of the material is useful and applicable to the new officers when they start their training. For instance, there is the science behind lift and drag. When the students practice stalls and spins a few months later,

they will understand what is happening to their aircraft. Some material will be more useful later in their careers, for instance, the characteristics of different types of wings and wing configurations, which is useful when evaluating adversary aircraft and estimating what sorts of performance attributes they possess in a given regime of flight.

The eleven classes that make up the aviation weather module treat the atmosphere and how aircraft operate in it. The terminal objective of the unit is stated as follows: "Upon completion of this unit of instruction, the Student Naval Aviator will demonstrate knowledge of meteorological theory enabling them [*sic*] to make intelligent decisions when confronted with various weather phenomena and hazards." If nothing else, it makes the students smart enough to avoid thunderstorms!

The aircraft engines and systems course covers ten class periods, teaching the different engine types and the theory behind their operation. It also surveys the fundamentals of the different systems that enable aircraft to operate: for example, hydraulic, electric, pneumatic, fuel, and lubrication. Even though the pilots will hardly be qualified as aircraft mechanics when they complete this module, they will have a good appreciation of the mechanical elements of their aircraft.

Aviation navigation is one of the most challenging courses in API. The students tackle the rudimentaries of navigating while aloft, including the principles of dead reckoning and how wind not corrected for will destroy even the most carefully crafted plans. They learn about other peculiar aspects of navigation, including magnetic variation and how to account for its effects. The CR-3 computer is introduced, and together with a compass and a straightedge the young officers learn how to plot a course on a chart (it is never called a "map"). All fleet aircraft are equipped with modern navigational equipment, but the basics learned here will make the students better pilots in their future careers.

The course on flight rules and regulations introduces the instructions and directives, both federal and Navy, by which the students will conduct their lives as pilots. The material is complex, and this class serves as merely an introduction, but it is information that will ultimately become very familiar. One point taught is that restrictions exist for a reason. They likely will hear the term "written in blood" several times. This is another way of saying, "This rule was written because someone died—it's intended to keep you from killing yourself the same way!"

"Pensacola—the cradle of naval aviation." These seaplane ramps were constructed soon after NAS Pensacola was established in 1914.

Flight physiology, that is, how the body reacts to the demanding environment of flight, is also part of the API curriculum. The stresses of night flying, unusual attitudes, high altitude, and "high-g" flight often cause a pilot's physiology to act in curious ways. Classroom instruction is the first step in learning how to safely deal with them while airborne.

API is not all classroom work; there is quite a bit of emphasis on the physical; swimming holding first place. Although the water work is not something that challenges a strong swimmer (i.e., someone with a varsity high school swimming background) those that are only marginally competent in the water and think that the U.S. Navy will teach them to swim well during API are mistaken. The student taking this course should already have a good grounding in swimming skills and must be very comfortable in the water.

Basic strokes are introduced, including the crawl (American), the breaststroke, the sidestroke, and the elementary backstroke. Not much time is spent on these

A cousin of the crash car dummy, this mannequin models the latest in water survival equipment.

29

exercises, as the students are expected to already be fairly decent swimmers. In fact, they will be required to don full flight gear and swim 200 yards using these different strokes. They are also taught to drownproof and tread water, both with and without flight gear. The instructors do a good job of teaching them how to use different pieces of flight equipment to improve buoyancy; for instance, the flight suit can be filled with air and used as a life preserver (perhaps the ultimate test of students' aquatic skills is the requirement to swim a mile in eighty minutes or less, while wearing a flight suit). Those who experience difficulty with their water work will be given extra instruction in the evenings or be held back for several weeks or more. In the end, if they cannot meet the requirements, the weak swimmers will be washed out of the program.

Following the initial rounding out of their water training, the students advance to more aviation-specific work. They are introduced to a variety of special devices that teach them to cope and survive if an aircraft mishap puts them into the water. These unique contraptions have a "Spanish inquisition goes poolside" look to them, and their purposes are not immediately evident until the classes begin. The students are taught how to disentangle themselves from a parachute in the event it collapses on top of them once they splash into the ocean. Conversely, they also practice what to do on a windy day in case they eject from the aircraft and their parachute drags them across the surface of the water. Students are also trained to pull themselves into a life raft when wearing full flight gear: this is not easy, and more often than not trainees

Once a naval aviator ejects from a tactical jet he will deploy his seat pan and life raft to prepare for a water landing. *USN/Gary Nichols*

While the students do not actually jump from aircraft to become parachute trained, they do perform a parasailing exercise underneath a parachute that puts them several hundred feet into the air. *USN/Chris Desmond*

An underwater perspective of the shallow-water trainer. *USN/Katrina Beeler*

finally collapse sputtering and breathless into the bottom of the rubber dinghy (in the future they will feel a definite empathy for upturned turtles).

Future flyers also learn how to roll out of a raft and sink it when a rescue helicopter arrives; there is always a danger that the raft might be pulled up into the rotors and cause the aircraft to crash. Students are shown the different pieces of equipment the helicopter rescue crew might use to pull them out of the water. Among them is the "horse collar," with which the students wrap a sling under their arms and across the chest and connect it to a cable. They are then winched out of the pool and up onto a platform. All the while they endure a torrential spray that simulates the rotor wash from the helicopter.

The students spend a good deal of time training on the shallow-water egress trainer, This is a long, metal, submerged cage with chairs mounted on top—out of the water. The chairs swivel to fall inside the cage and put the students underwater. The students are taught to hold their breath while finding a reference point to orient themselves. They then swim through the narrow cage until they leave at one end. After a few initial exposures they practice this exercise with blackout goggles—unable to see and relying on touch alone.

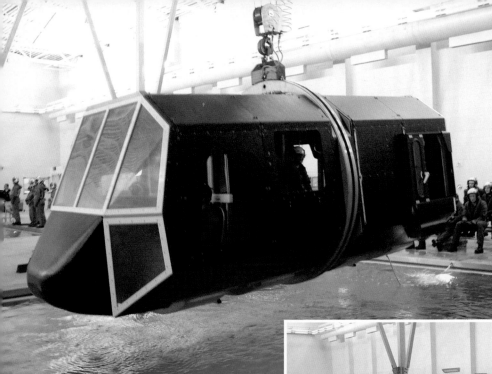

The helicopter dunker is perhaps the most intimidating piece of equipment in the pool.

It simulates a helicopter fuselage, and is primarily used to train students how to escape safely from a downed helicopter.

The dunker identifies those who lack the necessary composure to survive such emergencies in the real world.

Joint Training

Since the early 1990s the U.S. Navy has provided training for small numbers of U.S. Air Force air crews, while the U.S. Air Force has reciprocated by schooling small cadres of Navy and Marine flight students. Doing this increases the strengths of each service's training programs, and at the same time decreases costs and increases awareness and familiarity between the services. This is accomplished in part by taking advantage of aircraft, infrastructure, and instructor expertise so that in some cases one service does not need to entirely duplicate the capability of the other. Participation varies, but generally does not exceed 25 percent of any service's trainees. Students can volunteer for the program (although they are sometimes simply assigned).

Although no flight student of one service is entirely trained by the other branch, participating students do receive significant blocks of instruction from outside their own service. For instance, Navy and Marine students can receive their primary training on the T-6A Texan II at Moody AFB in Valdosta, Georgia, while U.S. Air Force students can receive their initial training on the T-34C, starting with API. Another option for Navy and Marine officers is primary training on the T-37B at Vance AFB in Enid, Oklahoma. The T-37 is perhaps the granddaddy of all U.S. trainers, having been in service since the mid-1950s. It is now being replaced by the T-6A Texan II.

All prospective U.S. Air Force C-130 pilots receive their multi-engine-aircraft training at NAS Corpus Christi, while all U.S. Navy students earmarked for the E-6 are trained at Vance AFB on the T-1. Nonpilot air crew programs also exist. Overall, the program has been relatively successful and it appears that it will remain in place for a while.

A successful student makes his way to the edge of the pool.

The work done on this trainer prepares the trainees for the multiplace helicopter dunker. This simulates a helicopter fuselage: it has multiple seating positions and can be lowered into the pool and manipulated until it is upside down. Its primary purpose is to train personnel to escape from a downed helicopter—but it also assists in identifying those students who do not have the composure or confidence to extricate themselves without panicking. As intimidating as the exercise is, however, there are very few students who cannot perform as expected.

Once seated in the dunker, the trainees are given a final briefing. They are to take a last, big gulp of air as the device fills with water, and at the same time they are supposed to find a handhold, or reference point. This last is essential

A view from the helo hoist platform. This student has successfully hooked himself into the "horse collar" and is preparing to be hauled out of the water.

because there is a real likelihood they will become disoriented once the entire contraption is totally submersed and turns upside down. Once all the movement stops, the students are expected to unstrap themselves, egress through a designated exit, swim to the surface, and then make their way to the edge of the pool.

Soon the trainees are expected to do the exercise a few more times wearing blacked-out goggles. They will again be totally reliant on their other senses to find their way clear of the dunker. The drill is tightly controlled, and safety swimmers are in the water at all times.

Beyond the pool, weather permitting, the students are put into the bay that runs the length of the base to practice some of what they have learned. After a description of the survival vest and the equipment commonly carried inside it, e.g., radios, flares, signal mirrors and knives, the students are given hands-on training with the equipment during a day of land survival instruction. They also learn to use the gear stashed inside ejection-seat kits and in the larger rafts carried aboard patrol and transport aircraft.

The hoist in operation.

The hoist as used in the real world. *USN/Daniel McLain*

Parasail training is always eagerly awaited. On this day the students, having learned the basics of parachute landing falls, are taken to a large open area. Individually, and in turn, they are harnessed to the open parachute attached by a very long rope to a pickup truck. On a signal the truck starts rolling into the wind. The student does his best to follow, at a run. Once the parachute is inflated and the trainee clears the ground and gets up to several hundred feet in the air, the attaching rope is released and the trainee floats to the ground, practicing what has been taught. As always, safety is paramount, but the entire evolution has a certain festiveness to it; everyone has a good time.

Although training in the water during API demands physical fitness, the syllabus also emphasizes fitness ashore. Cardiovascular and weight training is conducted, and the students also take classes in nutrition and cardiopulmonary resuscitation. Particular attention is given to health as it relates to aviation physiology. The class learns how the body reacts to the different regimes of flight, and also builds an awareness of the effects of diet and illness on an aviator's ability to perform.

One of the most interesting practical lessons related to aviation physiology is the time spent in the low-pressure chamber. During this carefully controlled exercise about fifteen to twenty students are put into a small sealed room. The pressure of the chamber is reduced to simulate an altitude of about 25,000 feet. In this circumstance the lungs cannot deliver enough oxygen to the brain to keep it functioning at full capacity. The students are directed to perform simple exercises like playing "pat-a-cake," or writing their own names over and over. The rapid degradation of their motor and cognitive skills soon becomes apparent, and the entire exercise quickly degenerates into giggling inaction. The danger posed by a loss of pressurization in an aircraft at high altitude is obvious. The students also learn some of the signals that the body sends when it suffers from a lack of oxygen, a condition known as hypoxia (e.g., tingling sensations in the extremities and thickening of the tongue, with the nails and lips turning blue).

The composition and content of the syllabus at API has proven effective over the years. The author found that there were very few substantial changes since he received the same outstanding instruction more than two decades earlier. By the time they have completed the course, the students have received an excellent foundation for their aviation careers. From API at Pensacola they will move on to primary training.

THREE

The dihedral designed into the T-6 II's wings is evident in this photograph. This slight upsweep makes the aircraft more stable—an important characteristic for a basic trainer.

Primary

The T-6 II is a newer design than the T-34C and that fact is apparent in this photograph.

At the conclusion of API the students progress to the primary phase (technically the Primary Multiservice Pilot Training System, or MPTS). This is a defining point in their training because it is where they will receive their first instruction on real Navy aircraft. It is also the start of a long journey; the T-34C, the T-37B, or the newer T-6A are the first of at least three different aircraft they will learn to fly no matter what career path they ultimately take, assuming that they successfully complete their training.

The U.S. Navy has been in the flight training business for nearly 100 years. Lieutenant T. G. Ellyson was the U.S. Navy's first aviator and received orders for flight instruction under the tutelage of Glenn Curtiss at North Island, San Diego, California. He first flew solo in 1911 when he became accidentally airborne for a few seconds during an exhibition. The short "flight" ended in a crash, and Ellyson started his career with more successful takeoffs than landings. He was eventually designated Naval Aviator No. 1 on March 4, 1913. The Marine Corps was not about to be left behind in this race to the skies, and Lieutenant Alfred A. Cunningham was the first Marine to receive flight

The T-6A Texan II

The U.S. Navy is replacing the T-34C with the Raytheon T-6A Texan II, a derivative of the Swiss Pilatus PC-9. The T-6A Texan II was one of several competitors for the Joint Primary Aircraft Training System, or JPATS. Both the Navy and the Air Force needed a replacement for their primary trainers, the T-34C and the T-37B respectively, and Raytheon was awarded the contract in 1996.

The new aircraft is a turboprop fitted with a four-bladed propeller driven by a 1,100-horsepower version of the same Pratt & Whitney Canada PT6A engine that powers the T-34C. It is a significantly advanced system compared with the types it is slated to replace, and incorporates ejection seats in a tandem arrangement that sit inside a pressurized cockpit under a sideways-opening canopy. The instrument panel is fitted with digital displays and an advanced avionics package, including GPS. The crew is supported with an onboard oxygen-generating system for flight at high altitudes.

The performance of the aircraft is impressive; it is capable of making nearly 300 knots and has a range of 900 nautical miles and a service ceiling of 31,000 feet. The up-rated engine helps it climb to 18,000 feet in less than six minutes. Its wingspan and fuselage length are nearly identical at just more than 33 feet each, and its basic empty weight is 6,500 pounds.

Both services are scheduled to continue to receive deliveries into the next decade. The U.S. Air Force began training student pilots with the Texan II in 2001 at Moody Air Force Base in Valdosta, Georgia. There, U.S. Navy and Marine Corps pilots train alongside their Air Force comrades. The Navy began training student NFOs with the type in 2003 at NAS Pensacola and should begin training pilots with the type at NAS Whiting and NAS Corpus Christi in the next several years. Total purchase of the T-6A II by both services is scheduled to exceed 700 airframes.

The original T-6 Texan, built by North American, was also a trainer used by both services and many other nations during World War II and into the 1950s. It helped to train nearly every U.S. military pilot during this period. The U.S. Navy knew the type by the SNJ designation, while Great Britain and the Commonwealth nations called it the Harvard.

It is interesting that two of the most important U.S. Navy trainers, the T-6A II and the T-45, are both derivatives of foreign aircraft.

instruction during 1912. He was designated as Naval Aviator No. 5.

Naval aviation continued to grow at a measured pace, and the U.S. Navy's first permanent air station was established at Pensacola, Florida, in 1914. Still, by the outbreak of World War I, the U.S. Navy and the Marine Corps combined had fewer than a hundred aircraft and pilots. The demands of the war changed this, and by the end of the conflict thousands of aviators were in training at several different air stations around the country. The nation's fledgling naval aviation arm distinguished itself by flying antisubmarine missions over both sides of the Atlantic. The Navy counted its first ace when 19-year-old Lieutenant (jg) David Ingalls was credited with six victories while flying a Sopwith Camel with the Royal Air Force 213 Squadron. Again, not to be outdone, the Marine Corps celebrated the award of the Medal of Honor to two of its fliers: Second Lieutenant Ralph Talbot and Gunnery Sergeant Robert Guy Robinson were recognized for their bravery over France.

Pictured here, Microsoft Flight Simulator 2002 is being used experimentally to help students become familiar with various aspects of flight training.

The interwar years saw naval aviation increase in size and importance. Still, it was a dangerous calling, and accidents claimed many lives during these "golden years" of aviation. Despite this being a time when new records were set at every turn, the maturation of new aviation technologies came at a cost. In fact, Lieutenant Ellyson—Naval Aviator No. 1—was killed over Chesapeake Bay in 1928. The Navy's training program was constantly racing to keep up with the new technologies while at the same time doing its best to emphasize safety and the preservation of human and physical assets. New aircraft and pilots were expensive.

The first U.S. aircraft carrier, the *Langley,* was converted from a collier (a coal ship) during 1923. By 1941, tactics and technology had evolved to the point where naval aircraft—employed appropriately—could project a nation's power across the globe. The Japanese proved this at Pearl Harbor.

The United States' entry into World War II demanded quantities of naval aircraft and the crews to fly them on a scale never before considered. In 1940 the U.S. Navy had fewer than 3,000 pilots on its rolls, a number that was pitifully inadequate to win the war. But across the country, seemingly overnight, airfields were built, flying schools were organized, industry was energized, and instructors were trained. Implemented and managed by the Navy, this vast training complex churned out nearly 60,000 high-quality pilots by the end of 1945 (naval aviation would never be so large again). Regardless, compared to today's records, it was not a clean or overly safe process: accident rates were high and thousands of aircraft and crews were lost.

But it got the job done; much of what was learned and developed during the war as it related to training pilots was retained and developed further, and today, those valuable techniques and lessons still form much of the basis of what is used.

Notwithstanding that naval aviation in the twenty-first century constitutes a team, those members who fly the aircraft are individuals—real people with real concerns, worries, and problems. With nearly a century of training aviators under its belt, the U.S. Navy takes this into account and has developed an institutional attitude that ensures the

There are different standards of dress and uniform among students and instructors as well as among services.

success of the individual students who are about to strap into its aircraft for the first time.

First, the U.S. Navy stresses that the greater part of success is the responsibility of the Student Naval Aviator (SNA). An excerpt from the FTI that introduces the students to the T-34C notes that they are the primary variable in their own success or failure:

The process by which a student is transformed into a skilled naval aviator is both complex and demanding. It can be accomplished only by intensive instruction, in the air as well as in the classroom. Success, for the most part, depends upon the student's attitude, cooperation, and attention to detail. The degree of skill attained by students depends largely upon their skill to understand new material and to work hard. Those students who cannot measure up to the high standards required throughout the various phases of training, because of either their lack of motivation or ability, must and will be attrited [sic].

The turbine engine T-34C has performed yeoman service since the late 1970s.

The Navy does its best to screen the young men and women who want to become aviators, and there is little doubt that those who get the nod are some of the brightest and most physically fit young people in the nation. Smarts and physical ability are not enough to ensure success, but focus, a positive attitude, and hard work will do a lot to get the average SNA through the program. Candidates who want to succeed have to submit to military discipline and be eager to participate and share with their classmates. Those who strike out on their own by showing a "lone-wolf" mentality cannot work as part of a team. The risk of washing out is much higher for the student who tries to go it alone.

When it comes to learning how to fly airplanes, there is no substitute for following established procedures. Just as there are so many ways to skin a cat, there are different ways to pilot an aircraft. But, the U.S. Navy has just one way to fly, "The Navy Way!" The standardization of procedures is utterly essential to efficient and safe operations, and the instructors who shape the new students will tolerate absolutely no deviations. This is reinforced through every aspect of training and builds on the discipline driven home at the academies or during OCS and ROTC.

Perhaps the most formal means by which standardization is maintained is the Naval Air Training and Operations Procedures Standardization Program, or NATOPS. The exact meaning of the acronym is forgotten almost immediately, but NATOPS very quickly becomes the professional bible of every naval aviator. New students immerse themselves in the appropriate books as they familiarize themselves with their new aircraft. Their commitment to memory of seemingly endless lists of emergency procedures and other hard data contained in the manuals is a grueling but necessary task that tests the best pupils.

Inside their hard, blue, plastic covers, the NATOPS manuals cover a wide range of aircraft types and relevant disciplines in depth. The material is often dry, and more than one student has nodded off while trying to cover the technical aspects. The generic nickname of any NATOPS manual is "big blue sleeping pill." Boring or not, though, it is a proven system responsible for much of the success that naval aviation enjoys today.

From the time SNAs commence API, grades become a dreaded but necessary part of their life. The grading systems are designed to appraise the trainees by a set of criteria to ensure that objectives are being met. But grades are also used to judge students against their peers. Because grades play a critical role in determining to which aircraft or community the student will ultimately be assigned, the competition among some of the best young people in the nation going through very arduous courses is fierce.

The primary phase is the first time that the SNAs will be graded on their flying performance. Because they carry more weight in the final analysis than academic grades, the flying marks are very important and the students worry about them, sometimes to the point that their anxiety undermines their ability to perform. Their apprehension is understood, and such platitudes as "if you worry about learning, the grades take care of themselves" are used to ameliorate the situation. But the students know that some instructors are more exacting than others, or that bad weather can make it more difficult to perform, or that some schedules are more challenging than others. In fact there are a number of factors that influence what grades are awarded. In the end—for the most part—everything averages out over time, and the grades are a fairly true appraisal of the individuals' performance.

Of course, the SNAs receive their grades from the instructors they fly with. These officers are aviators who have completed one or more flying tours in the fleet and have the requisite experience to be effective teachers. Most of the instructors in the primary phase come from the helicopter or multi-engine community, as most of

The instructor is ultimately responsible for the aircraft and the safe conduct of the flight.

A lineup of T-34C propellers. Note that the blade tips are painted yellow on one side and red and white on the other. These markings delineate the arc of the propeller when it is turning and are intended to reduce accidents on the flight line.

This photograph shows a fairly typical aspect of a training command flight line where rows of aircraft cover the ramp.

the instructors with a tactical jet background teach the tactical strike syllabus in the T-45 trainer.

They all have completed a specialized course that teaches them to be effective mentors. The students soon learn that they can expect to do well and satisfy their requirements so long as they have thoroughly prepared for their scheduled period of instruction regardless of a instructor's reputation or demeanor. It is also important that the SNA is open and receptive to criticism: an instructor cannot be effective without being critical. The T-34C FTI contains a paragraph that neatly encapsulates the attitude that SNAs should embrace while going through flight training:

Remember one important thing for as long as you fly an aircraft: You must be your own most aggressive critic. This does not mean that you become a mental case in the cockpit, but it does mean that as an aviator beginning the flight training syllabus, you must demonstrate one of the most critical qualities a professional aviator has: self-discipline. This means that you prepare for every hop as if your professional reputation is at stake. Your flights are not contests where someone is keeping score and counting your mistakes. Your flight grades should not be as important as your own honest appraisal of your flight performance. You are expected to come well prepared, but you must expect to make mistakes. Most of these mistakes are forgiven as long as you deal with them professionally, on the spot, and learn from them. That is why they call this flight training.

Students entering the primary phase soon learn that classroom instruction does not end with API. Once that course of instruction is complete, the students travel only a short distance from Pensacola to NAS Whiting Field—also on the Florida panhandle—or to NAS Corpus Christi in southern Texas to begin the primary phase. A few will

The control stick of the T-6A is nearly as sophisticated as that of top-of-the-line fighters.

The throttle, or power control lever, grip for the T-6A is quite like that of a fighter and includes the control for the speedbrake and the microphone switch for the radio.

be selected for training with the U.S. Air Force in either the T-37 or T-6A Texan II (those courses of training will be addressed later). Classroom instruction continues with special emphasis on the Navy's primary trainer, the T-34C.

This aircraft originated from the civilian Model 35 Beechcraft and the U.S. Navy operated a piston engine development of that type: The T-34B. Pleased with the aircraft's simplicity and handling characteristics, the Navy nevertheless wanted a more powerful primary trainer that better emulated the turbojet-powered aircraft to which students would advance. The turboprop powered T-34C's capabilities inspire envy in most civilian, general-aviation pilots. It carries a student and instructor in a tandem arrangement and can exceed 250 knots and reach an altitude of 25,000 feet. With a wingspan of just over 33 feet and a length of nearly 29 feet, the aircraft has a range in excess of 600 nautical miles. With an unpressurized cockpit, it is equipped with oxygen equipment for flight above 10,000 feet.

The PT-6A-25 engine that powers the T-34C is fitted with a torque limiter that purposely keeps the engine from producing more than 56 percent of its available power. This lengthens engine life and makes the aircraft more manageable for the fledgling fliers. In service, the engine has proven tremendously reliable—a great credit to its manufacturer, Pratt & Whitney of Canada.

Before the SNAs ever step out onto the ramp, they are put through rigorous drills in 2C42 cockpit procedural trainers (CPTs), as well as 2B37 flight simulators. The CPTs are simpler, less expensive devices than the flight simulators, and are used primarily for procedural training. The flight simulators allow the student to practice various maneuvers without using the actual aircraft. This provides tremendous cost savings to the U.S. Navy and permits the SNAs to make mistakes—and learn from them—before ever getting close to real aircraft.

The day finally arrives when the new pupils are scheduled for their first sortie in the T-34C. Strong students will be

The T-6A Texan II is a modern design. Its advanced cockpit, pressurized cabin, ejection seats and, most of all, its performance, are much more like those of a fighter than the T-34C.

"What's this do? What's that do? How about that cable?"

well prepared, having memorized all the requirements not only for this first flight, but also for the next one or two. (This is a necessity because last-minute scheduling changes may make extra aircraft or instructors available, and the students are expected to be ready and prepared to take advantage of these windfalls, particularly if the option presents itself to fly a second event during a given day.) Aside from classroom and simulator instruction, aggressive students will have gotten informal debriefings from classmates or others who have just completed the same event. The idea is not only to keep the newest students from making the same mistakes, but also to capitalize on what worked. It will not be long until these latest students provide the same sort of information and help to those who follow. An institutionalized practice in Navy training is that students, regardless of the course or instruction, always "cooperate to graduate" whenever possible.

At the assigned briefing time the students meet their instructors at the squadron ready room (the author was late for his very first T-34C event in 1981—he had waited more than an hour at the wrong squadron, a victim of bad gouge!). Instructors and students cover the material for that day's sortie together. All the information should be familiar to the new fliers, but in the context of a real flying event it usually makes more sense than when it was presented in the classroom. After the brief, the crews check their aircraft assignment and "suit up" before reviewing their aircraft's maintenance log, the aircraft discrepancy book (ADB, explained in detail in Chapter 4). When satisfied with the maintenance record of their aircraft, it is time to step out onto the parking ramp.

Particularly at Whiting Field, the huge number of neatly parked and identically painted orange-and-white T-34Cs can be overwhelming. Nevertheless, there is a method to the seeming madness that is the sea of aircraft, and the instructors explain the layout of the ramp and how to find a particular aircraft. For their part, the students usually feel a bit self-conscious and vulnerable on the flight line. Flight suits, boots, and helmets are all new and stiff, and the life-preserving unit feels awkward and heavy.

Instructors are careful to teach the neophytes the basics of safety on the ramp, or flight line, which is an extraordinarily dangerous and unforgiving environment. Every aircraft features a three-bladed propeller that can turn a living, walking human being into a wet solution of blood, ground bone, and flesh in a fraction of a second. Instructors stress always being on guard and demand that the pupils keep their heads on a swivel. For their part, the students, like bear cubs who never wander far from their mother, stay close to the experienced aviator. With time they will gain more confidence, but will always treat any ramp as if it were infested with poisonous snakes.

At the aircraft the instructor and student perform the preflight check together. First, from a distance, they look the entire aircraft over to make certain that there is no obvious damage or significant leaks, and that no panels are missing. Also, they ensure that no large objects such as fire extinguishers or stepladders are in a position to block their path when the time comes to taxi for takeoff. At the aircraft they

A student preflights the rudder of a T-34C.

Preflight inspections are not just for the training command.

45

Instruction takes place everywhere, including the flight line.

greet the plane captain, who is a ground crew member responsible for preparing the aircraft for flight and assisting the crew during start and post-start procedures. The plane captain will point out any discrepancies discovered. Then there is a very careful and detailed scrutiny of nearly every accessible item on the aircraft. (Although this first inspection is done with the instructors, students are subsequently expected to do a very complete and thorough preflight check on their own. As they progress through the syllabus they will be quizzed more and more on the details of the aircraft components until their knowledge of the T-34C is nearly encyclopedic.)

With the preflight check complete, the instructor helps the student strap into the aircraft. The young flier takes some comfort in the fact that the cockpit looks exactly the same as the simulator that he has "flown" several times already. Nonetheless, the flight line has a different feel and sound and smell than does the simulator building, and the student must concentrate carefully when going through the checklists. Working with the plane captain is a new experience, and the student exchanges tentative signals with him during the startup procedures. Reassuringly, the engine fires up just as it did during simulator training. The value of the simulator can hardly be overstated.

Radio communication in a busy military environment is a new experience, and initially the neophyte aviator very often feels intimidated. There is a great deal of

Beyond primary training . . . larger aircraft demand bigger doses of caution. This F/A-18 sits much higher off the ground than the aircraft in the training command.

chatter on the radio, and the student must pick precisely the right time to speak, and listen carefully for a reply so as to not "garbage up" the airwaves with requests for clarification. At the same time the student wants to project a professional image—half of being "cool" is sounding good on the radio.

Few people do it cleanly the first time, but after some coaching from the instructor the student gets a flight clearance for the sortie as well as permission to taxi. The instructor demonstrates, or "demos," how to taxi while the

student observes the technique as well as the hand signals from the plane captain. Almost every maneuver on the first flight is demonstrated before the student tries it alone. Taxiing is not very difficult, and after a few flights it will come as second nature.

At the end of the runway, or hold-short area, the student goes over the takeoff checklist before calling for takeoff clearance. Once received, the instructor positions the aircraft onto the runway, makes a few final checks—including a wipeout, a quick confirmation that all the

The T-6A's aft cockpit is optimized for instructor duty. Here the elevated position is obvious; this is especially valuable during landing practice when it is crucial for the instructor to be able to see over the nose of the aircraft.

In contrast, the T-34C's aft cockpit is not appreciably elevated above the front cockpit.

flight controls are free and operating—and advances the power control lever (PCL). The propeller bites into the air and tries to pull the aircraft forward; after a quick review of the engine instruments, the instructor releases the brakes and lets the aircraft roll, and a few seconds later the ship is airborne.

Thanks to the SNA's initial flight instruction as part of Introductory Flight Screening the sensation of being airborne in a small craft is not completely foreign even though the T-34C is quite a bit more powerful than the general-aviation airplanes the student flew earlier. So it demands more attention and respect because its performance can get the beginning pilot into trouble more quickly.

This is a fairly unremarkable photograph except for the fact that the author flew this exact same aircraft almost 23 years prior to the day he captured this image.

Before long the instructor hands over the controls and the student tries piloting the aircraft. Because the T-34C is inherently stable yet still responsive, it is not long before the pupil begins to feel comfortable with the aircraft in gentle turns, climbs, and descents. While the aircraft's instrumentation and general handling characteristics are very similar to what the 2B37 device simulates, the general consensus is that the actual aircraft is easier to fly. While the student strives to gain familiarity with the aircraft, the instructor points out landmarks that the student needs to learn in order to navigate the local area. At the same time the student practices and reviews in-flight checklists and procedures. With so much going on, it seems as if only a short time passes before the instructor directs the student to turn the aircraft back toward home base. During the return flight the course rules required for recovery to the base are introduced. To the student they seem almost impossibly complex.

Approaching the airfield the instructor takes control of the aircraft to introduce the "break," or overhead entry. It is the quickest way to get multiple aircraft into the landing pattern, and the normal way of doing business in the fleet—especially at the aircraft carrier. This is the student's first exposure to any real additional gravitational pull ("g") created by a hard turn. The instructor aligns the aircraft with the runway and once overhead snaps it into a hard four-g turn until, after 180 degrees, it is pointed in the opposite direction and offset to one side of the runway. If the student has not gotten prepared by tensing his muscles, he may well pass out as gravity pulls the blood from the head down into the body. Regardless, this initial exposure will probably leave the student light-headed for a few seconds.

In that short time the instructor has already lowered the landing gear and flaps to prepare the aircraft for landing. After a quick review of the landing checklist the instructor commences a descending turn toward the end

Past Training

Training is different now than it was during the early days of World War II. Hamilton McWhorter was an aviation cadet training at NAS Pensacola when Japan attacked Pearl Harbor on December 7, 1941. In his book, *The First Hellcat Ace,* he recalls how the already rigorous training schedule was stepped up:

Hamilton McWhorter in World War II.

> Almost immediately, the training schedule shifted to an eight-day week—we trained for eight straight days, then had a day off. Also, the workdays stretched to ten or twelve hours, rather than the eight-hour days we had gotten used to.

The demands of the new regimen contributed to an already high—by contemporary standards—accident rate. McWhorter recalls:

> The next day, Sunday, there were five fatal accidents. Most of them involved cadets who just flew straight into the ground. . . . One evening, the personal effects from the of the boys' bodies was brought back. Someone showed me his room key, which had been in his pocket when he crashed. He had hit the ground so hard that the key was bent at a ninety-degree angle.

> Still, the training was excellent. McWhorter became the first U.S. Navy pilot to score five kills while flying the F6F Hellcat, and ultimately finished the war with twelve aerial victories to his credit.

T-34C operations at NAS Corpus Christi go on nearly continuously during clear weather. Here, one crew prepares to taxi while in the background another practices touch and go landings.

During a typical contact, or familiarization, flight, the T-34 student will fly a dizzying number of touch-and-go landings.

of the runway, while explaining exactly what is being done with the aircraft and what the student should be paying attention to. A few seconds later, the tires emit a quiet chirp as the instructor demonstrates a perfect touchdown. After rolling on the hard surface for just an instant, he advances the PCL and the aircraft leaps into the air again.

Once he has put a few hundred feet between the aircraft and the ground, the instructor passes the controls to the student and gives instructions to turn downwind; it is the student's turn. It is likely that this first attempt will be an awkward and sorry replication of the instructor's landing. However, after a few more efforts the tempo begins to

A T-34C flies past the runway duty officer (RDO) cart at NAS Whiting Field.

make sense. By that time, though, the sortie is over, and the instructor retakes the controls for the final landing.

After parking the aircraft and completing all the post-flight paperwork, the instructor and student sit down for a thorough debriefing. This is arguably the most important part of the day's event. It is where the student will receive exhaustive comments on performance: what was done right, what needs more work, and what could be done differently or better. It is also where the student can take the time to ask more detailed questions. While it is possible to get clarification on some maneuvers or procedures while airborne, the dynamic environment of flight and the constraints of the cockpit setting sometimes make comprehensive instruction or critiquing difficult. So the debriefing is when the student takes advantage of the instructor's expertise to clear up any misunderstandings. There is no good reason for an SNA to complete a flight event without a clear idea about what occurred or what is about to in the next few events.

Weather permitting, the flow of events continues at a quick pace. The student's basic flying skills improve with each sortie, and a steady sequence of new maneuvers is introduced in every successive flight. Not only are basic turns and climbs and descents introduced, but so are

A solo student looks over his right shoulder down an intersecting runway.

Landing practice during the early evening hours is often easier for the students because there is less wind and turbulence.

Note the pocket checklist on the glareshield of this T-34C; there is no desk in the cockpit of the T-34C, nor in most U.S. Navy aircraft.

stalls and emergency procedures. It will not be long before the instructor pulls back the PCL and—with the aircraft dropping out of the sky—demands that the student react exactly according to the prescribed procedures appropriate for either a low-altitude power loss or a high-altitude power loss. The student must go through the procedures by memory, while simultaneously maneuvering the aircraft to put it down in a spot that will do the minimum damage to him and the instructor, the aircraft, and whatever might be on the ground. It is only just before touchdown that the instructor will take the controls, add power, and fly the two of them away from whatever surface the student was about to touch down on.

One of the most challenging aspects of flight is landing the aircraft safely. Shooting an arrow is easy, but hitting the center of the target is difficult. Likewise, taking off in an airplane is easy, but touching down precisely is very demanding. Even under normal circumstances it can be trying, but the Navy knows that circumstances are not often normal. The student will be taught to land with various combinations of flaps, during crosswinds, and with various simulated engine or propeller malfunctions. Fliers must always be prepared and trained to get the aircraft back as long as it can be flown. For this reason a significant portion of every sortie is spent at the airfield.

There are procedures and more procedures, emergencies and more emergencies, and combinations of procedures in conjunction with combinations of emergencies. It is not too long before the flying and navigation portions of sorties

The warped skin, dirt, and exhaust on the side of this T-34C highlight some of the fatigue that the aircraft has endured over its service life.

This T-34C is flying quite low and has yet to make it over the runway. Still, the aircraft is a responsive yet forgiving trainer, and instructors feel comfortable in giving the students free rein.

come almost instinctually, while the procedural conduct of flights becomes almost too much to deal with.

It does not take long, though, before students demonstrate a level of competence that is reassuring to both themselves and their instructors. By the time SNAs have twelve sorties under their belt, it is time for the "safe for solo" check flight. Obviously this is an important event to the students; failure to pass the flight will preclude them from soloing and advancing through the syllabus until receiving more instruction. The Navy's official stance on all check flights is that students should not dwell too much on the significance of the event, but should simply be prepared for the flight just as for any other. The T-34C FTI has this to say about check rides:

> The student should place no special significance on designated check flights and should not anticipate failure if a superlative performance is not demonstrated. The designated check flight is merely an evaluation by another instructor of the evaluations other instructors have given the student. If a student fails to meet the accepted standards of progress, the instructor will grade the student's performance unsatisfactory rather than allow him to continue ahead in the syllabus. The check pilot is obligated to judge the student fairly in comparison with accepted standards.

An instructor is in the front cockpit of this T-34C, which is not the usual positioning. *USN/Rich Stewart*

Left: The T-37, or "Tweet," is the Air Force's equivalent of the T-34C, and is the oldest trainer in use by U.S. forces today—dating from the mid-1950s. *USAF*

A small number of U.S. Navy and Marine students do their primary training on the T-37 at Vance Air Force Base in Enid, Oklahoma as part of the joint training program. *USAF*

As can be imagined, this statement does little to ease the pre-check-flight jitters. To be fair, there is little that Navy officialdom can say or do to soothe nerves in this sort of circumstance; the students are either good enough to progress or they are not. The check flight is intended to determine which.

But the training is good and most students pass this event with little trouble. Their reward is a solo flight during which they are allowed to take an aircraft to the working areas and practice maneuvers at their own pace and under no scrutiny. For most SNAs, the notion of being alone in the aircraft takes a bit of getting used to, but they

quickly find that the aircraft fly just the same regardless of whether anyone is watching them or not. After practicing some basic air work, the students are allowed to go to one of the outlying training fields where they can further refine their landing skills before bringing the aircraft back to home base. This event, aside from being a "good deal," is a confidence builder that validates the students' own hard work as well as the money and resources that the service has invested in them.

A phase of flight eagerly anticipated by many students is the introduction of aerobatics. This part of the syllabus follows the solo flight and introduces the SNAs to such

This Marine Corps Harrier pilot has mastered formation flight. Aerial refueling requires smooth and precise control inputs. Poor weather and darkness can make the task much more difficult. *USMC/Paul Leicht*

A nice front-quarter and profile view of the T-34C. The turbine-powered T-34C has provided excellent service since the 1970s.

Formation flying is introduced in the T-6A just as it is in the T-34C and T-37. *USAF/Jeffrey Allen*

The S-3 Viking's primary role during the Cold War was antisubmarine warfare. Since then the S-3 has taken on other roles. The S-3 flying the lead position in this photograph is equipped with a Harpoon anti-shipping missile. *USN/Chris Valdez*

classic maneuvers as the loop, the aileron roll, the barrel roll, and the Immelmann turn. It is excellent for those who have never had the opportunity to experience this sort of physically and mentally demanding three-dimensional flight regime. Their reactions tell whether or not they are suited for the type of flying that they will encounter while flying tactical jets, or if they have a temperament that is better for less dynamic aircraft and missions.

Each SNA takes to this aspect of the training differently—and not always predictably. Sometimes the hard-bitten jock who has declared since the beginning that he will be a fighter pilot finds that he has no stomach whatsoever for high-g flight. Conversely, the most bookish student may find a real talent for the inverted twisting and turning and relatively high-g flight that make some of the most aggressive students pale.

Students are also introduced to instrument flying during the primary phase. Naval aviation operates in some of the worst weather conditions known, and its pilots must be proficient in all aspects of instrument flight. Fortunately, the

The U.S. Navy emphasizes standard landing pattern procedures.

Inside a pressurized cockpit with an oxygen mask clamped over his face—and strapped into an ejection seat—this T-6A student looks like he could be sitting inside any number of modern, high-performance fighters.

inherent stability of the T-34C as well as its avionics suite, including a GPS navigation system, makes it an ideal instrument trainer.

Just as the SNAs received extensive classroom and simulator instruction in familiarization, or "contact" training before advancing to their first T-34C flight, they receive additional classroom instruction and simulator experience before attempting their first instrument flight. The theory and science behind instrument flight is not instinctive, and the classroom instruction is backed up with various texts and publications, as well as computer-based aids. Still, it is not until the students get into the simulator for individual lessons that the application of instrument flying begins to make real sense.

When the SNAs get to the aircraft for actual sorties, they typically fly underneath a hood in the rear seat; it is where the term "blind flying" takes on real meaning. Here they are able to actually practice what they have learned. The training, which comprises basic instrument and radio instrument sorties, includes various types of instrument approaches and departures and en route navigation and

A student checks the area to his right before he taxis his T-34C out of its parking spot. Note the red and white markings that delineate the aircraft's propeller arc.

procedures. And of course, the students practice all manner of emergencies, including recoveries from unusual attitudes as well as navigation using an instrument suite that is only partially functional. Although they will receive their instrument ratings during later stages, while flying

The instructor in the rear seat of this T-34C watches carefully as his student taxis toward the runway. The light-colored shroud behind the instructor is an instrument hood.

different types of aircraft, this initial instruction during MPTS gives them a very solid foundation for later flying.

There is instruction in night flight that builds on what is taught in the familiarization and instrument phases. Night flight can be difficult for the young pilots: nothing really changes but everything looks different. Because visual cues inside and outside the cockpit are diminished, there is a certain amount of fumbling that makes operations slower. Nevertheless, naval aviation does not stop just because the sun drops below the horizon, and proficiency during night operations must come without conscious thought. Indeed, the increasing sophistication of sensors—both friendly and enemy— makes combat a reality twenty-four hours a day. Again, this training, although it hardly gives the SNAs the level of competence and confidence that will ultimately be required of them, provides a good foundation for later instruction.

One of the last stages of primary instruction is formation flying. Tactical jets and helicopters, and sometimes even larger platforms, often operate as part of a group or other formation of aircraft. Even getting somewhere, in the case of fighters needing to refuel from airborne tankers, requires formation-flying skills. And perhaps most importantly, killing the enemy is done more efficiently in a group rather than as a stream of individual aircraft.

"Gouge"

"Hey, what's the gouge on? . . ." It's as common a phrase in naval aviation lingo as any other. "Gouge" is informal data or information that students share in order to get through the syllabus with less hassle and better results. Thorough and official instruction is provided by the U.S. Navy through various manuals and course books; gouge, however, fills in the small voids that can leave students scratching their heads.

Gouge may be as simple as delineating the best way to get scheduled for extra simulator time, or as complex as a detailed explanation of the theory behind calculating a TACAN point-to-point solution in high-crosswind situations. It may describe the best way to handle a particularly picky instructor, or it may attempt to map out which aircraft type assignments are expected during the coming year. It can be as informal or simple as passing handwritten classroom notes from one student to another or as sophisticated as a web site. It can cover almost anything.

But it can be dangerous. As the old saying has it: "If you live by the gouge, you must be prepared to die by the gouge." This means that students should not rely solely on the shortcut that gouge often is, but instead should use gouge to complement what they already have learned from officially sanctioned sources. As all naval aviators have learned at one time or another in their careers, "There's plenty of bad gouge out there," and it has, does, and will get the unwary fliers in trouble.

Naval aviators learn the rudiments of formation-flying during MPTS. In their T-34Cs they practice the basics as two-ship flights. At first, the notion is a foreign and sometimes frightening one; there is a fear—a real one—that a wrong move might send one's own propeller thrashing into the airframe of a wingman or flight lead. Nevertheless, the students master these fears under good and competent instruction and soon they become, if not expert, a little less uncomfortable with the challenge of flying close to another aircraft. With only a few feet between the two airframes, the students learn procedures, the basics of changing positions, lead changes, join-ups, and dynamic maneuvering as a flight. They will refine these skills later in their training and they will use them to bring the battle to the enemy.

After several months of classroom, simulator, and flight instruction, the time finally arrives when the SNAs complete the syllabus. The average students will have flown fifty flights, spending more than 100 flight hours aloft, and will have a solid grounding in basic flight skills, instrument flying, night flying, aerobatics, and formation flying. Students will be thoroughly indoctrinated into NATOPS and will have demonstrated the good judgment, and procedural and technical competence that the U.S. Navy requires.

Formation flying is introduced in the primary phase. *USN*

FOUR

This student has flown a good approach. His arresting hook will engage a cable in just an instant.

T-45 Part 1

Not everyone makes it through the primary phase. Of those who finish the API syllabus, approximately 10 percent fail to complete primary flight training. There are many causes for failure, and the reasons include those that can be reasonably predicted and many that cannot. For instance, despite their comprehensive nature, the rigorous medical screenings are not infallible, and a few officers are found to be physically unfit for flying after they start training. Additionally, some students lack the spatial aptitude or the eye-hand coordination that the program demands, while others simply discover that a career as a naval aviator—for one reason or another—is not what they desire. For the most part, these former flight students, or "fallen angels," are assigned to other occupational specialties and become first-rate contributors to their respective services.

The students who do finish primary flight training in the T-34C, the T-37B, or the T-6A receive orders to continue instruction in one of six training syllabuses. Those who have been selected to fly tactical jet aircraft proceed to either NAS Meridian, Mississippi, or NAS Kingsville, Texas, for instruction in the T-45 Goshawk. The T-45 is a derivative of the British Aerospace (BAE) T.1 Hawk—an advanced, two-seat jet trainer that became operational with the Royal Air Force (RAF) in 1976. Since that time,

A T-45 is framed by the blue position light atop the Landing Signal Officer's platform as it approaches the aircraft carrier.

this very capable aircraft has evolved considerably and currently serves with a number of air forces around the world as not only a trainer but as a light attack jet.

At about the same time that the Hawk entered service with the RAF, the U.S. Navy was floating a proposal that called for a single aircraft to replace both the T-2C Buckeye and the TA-4J Skyhawk: the service's intermediate and advanced trainers, respectively. The two jets were beginning to age, and the service recognized that a single aircraft that could meet the full spectrum of strike-training needs

Fallen Angels

One of the earliest and most famous of the "Fallen Angels" was Marine Corps General Lewis B. "Chesty" Puller. After several years of distinguished service in Haiti just after World War I, Puller was commissioned as a regular officer and soon after received orders to flight school. He was enamored with the image of the "Knight in the Sky."

But he failed to complete the syllabus. Reconciling himself to the fact that he had little aptitude for flight, he returned to the infantry and further service in Central America and China. He eventually sealed his reputation in the Pacific during World War II as one of the most beloved and toughest leaders the Marine Corps has ever known. Later, during the Korean War and the retreat from the Chosin Reservoir, Puller was informed that he was surrounded by several Chinese divisions and that his supplies were cut off. "Good," he is quoted as saying, "They've got us right where we want 'em. We can shoot in every direction now!" Puller eventually retired with more than fifty decorations, including five Navy Crosses, which is ranked only behind the Medal of Honor in the precedence of awards for bravery.

would be more efficient and less costly than maintaining and operating two separate types. Accordingly, BAE teamed with McDonnell Douglas to propose an aircraft carrier–capable version of the basic Hawk aircraft. This submission was one of many put forward by various aircraft manufacturers. The Navy was impressed with the Hawk's potential, and in 1981 the design that ultimately became the T-45 Goshawk was selected.

It was not an easy birth. Converting a land design for operations aboard an aircraft carrier has always been a difficult process, and this effort was no different. The manufacturing team (McDonnell Douglas was the prime contractor) struggled to overcome unfavorable stall characteristics, poor engine response, difficult ground handling, high approach speeds, and stability deficiencies. Many of these problems were a result of changes made to the basic airframe in order to make it suitable for Navy operations. Some of the major differences between the original Hawk design and the T-45 included new wings with leading-edge slats, redesigned vertical and horizontal stabilizers, speed brakes moved to the sides of the fuselage, a reworked landing gear, and an arresting hook.

Nevertheless, nearly all the challenges were overcome, and students began training operationally on the type in 1994—thirteen years after the design was selected. Despite the development difficulties, the aircraft has proved a success and has flown more than half a million hours. It is a safe and relatively forgiving trainer, but at the same time it possesses the performance characteristics required to prepare students to fly front-line fighter and attack aircraft.

Upon arrival at their new assignment, the students go through the drill of administrative processing while they prepare for academic training. Typically, the sky overhead the base is swarming with aircraft, and a faint scent of burned jet fuel permeates the air. It is a smell that will become a part of their lives just as much as the fragrance of fresh-cut wood perfumes the world of the carpenter.

The T-45 is a real jet. As well suited as the turboprop-powered T-34C is for primary training, it is not a sexy machine. After all, Tom Cruise did not sit behind a propeller in *Top Gun*. In contrast to the basic trainers, the T-45 looks

This student is studying before a simulator session.

Simulator instruction is generally given by former military aviators who typically have thousands of flight hours and a long career in naval aviation, much of it in combat.

like a bona fide combat aircraft—mostly because it is. Even in their white-and-orange paint, the jets have a certain dynamism about them. During primary training some students feel slightly self-conscious when they send home photos of themselves standing in front of the T-34C, which is a bit like posing with rubber training pants. At Kingsville and Meridian, however, there is no hesitation posting pictures of themselves with the T-45.

However, it will be several weeks before the newly arrived students will be allowed to climb into one of the sleek jets for actual flight training. Academic drills come first.

The T-45 is unique in that it was the first training aircraft selected as only part of an entire package. In fact, Boeing (which bought McDonnell Douglas in 1997) calls

its concept the "T-45 Training System," or "T-45 TS." The system is made up of five elements: the aircraft, a computer-assisted instruction program, advanced flight simulators, a computerized training integration system, and a contractor logistics support package.

Although traditional classroom instruction is still an important part of the syllabus, students complete much of their academic training with computer-assisted programs. While lacking some of the character of a "warm-bodied" instructor, the technology-based tutoring allows the students to learn at a pace that is more tailored to their own requirements. It also permits them to revisit difficult-to-understand subject matter without interrupting or holding back an entire class. Additionally, they can review

This early simulator type was used to train thousands of aviators during and after World War II. Note that its chassis is made of wood--a concession to wartime metal conservation efforts.

Students do not normally wear their flight gear in the simulator during the T-45 syllabus, but the simulator events are otherwise very similar to an actual flight. Here, a student prepares to strap on a kneeboard, which holds many of his checklists. Note the worn paint on the canopy bow where thousands of students have used it as a handhold to lower or raise themselves into or out of the cockpit.

The instrument panel of a T-45A. Although this is a photograph of the simulator, even an expert eye would not be able to distinguish it from an actual aircraft mostly because the panel is made up of the same components.

whatever instruction they need as often as they desire and whenever they prefer.

Just as they had to devote a great deal of time to learning the different systems and subsystems that made up their aircraft during primary training, the students once again are required to dedicate many hours of study in order to become intimately familiar with the T-45. Still, they enjoy one of the benefits that the U.S. Navy anticipated when it replaced the T-2C and the TA-4J with the T-45: they have to learn only one jet rather than two.

It is just as well because the T-45 comprises so many components and elements that it takes time and serious effort to know them all thoroughly. Not only must the students become experts on the aircraft's mechanical and electronic systems, but they must also become familiar with the T-45's performance numbers and handling characteristics, not to mention the quirks and idiosyncrasies that help color the personality of the aircraft.

To say that the syllabus is intensively academic is perhaps an understatement. In total, there are more than sixty separate lesson and lecture guides, workbooks, instructions, and other documents. A handful of them are modest in size, of only a few dozen pages or so. Most are more robust; the air combat maneuvering (ACM) lecture guide has 272 pages. Predictably, very soon the excitement at the prospect of flying the T-45 is tempered by the seemingly cruel task of absorbing the mountain of academic material. It is one of those points in the syllabus where students experience a higher than normal level of anxiety and self-doubt.

Still, the new arrivals need only look around to realize that classes made up of students just like them are successfully negotiating the curriculum. It takes only some quiet reflection to realize that the U.S. Navy wants them to succeed (indeed, the Navy cannot afford for them to not succeed) and that they would not be there if they did not have the skills to fly the syllabus through to completion.

Those students who passed through the primary phase flying the T-34C have had no experience with an ejection seat and have yet to be fitted with the requisite harness—a necessity for crewing the T-45 because it is equipped with a very modern and capable ejection seat. Sometime during their first few weeks of training they will make the trip to the flight equipment shop, where they will be measured and sewn into one of the custom-made torture devices. A confusing snake's nest of hard nylon

straps and metal buckles, the harness can twist itself into a tangled mess in an instant, and it can take bewildered novices half an hour to untangle and don it correctly. But like many things, practice and familiarity will make things right. In a few months the harness will slip on in seconds, and the fit will be like a lambskin glove.

Along with the harness, students will be fitted with a g-suit. Part clothing, part device, the g-suit is a much-modified pair of trousers that squeezes the pilot's legs and lower torso to keep blood in the upper body during high-g maneuvers. Bladders in the suit fill with air through a hose that connects the suit to the aircraft. Blood is drained more slowly from the brain during hard turns, and this helps to keep the pilot from going unconscious. It is a design that dates from World War II and has undoubtedly saved millions of dollars in aircraft and many lives.

Aside from T-45-specific instruction, much of what the students are initially taught is a rehash of what they

A T-45 student wings his simulator over a synthetic, South Texas landscape. The instrumentation accurately reproduces that of the real aircraft.

The student in the rear seat of this T-45 is pulling "the bag" over the top of his cockpit. He is getting ready to get airborne on an instrument flight and the shroud will cut off all visual cues to the outside world.

learned in Pensacola. Aerodynamics is emphasized again as is meteorology and the principles of instrument flight. Because they will receive an instrument rating during their training on the T-45, it is absolutely essential that the students be thoroughly prepared to operate fast jets in and among civilian air traffic in the nation's airspace.

Between the classroom and the real jet is the flight simulator, or "the box." (Many of aviation's early simulators were indeed box-shaped contraptions, and the name has stuck through the years.) The T-45 device, officially known as the 2F137 instrument flight trainer, is a near-exact replica of the aircraft's cockpit. It allows instructors to familiarize students with the aircraft's instrumentation and normal flight procedures without having to tie up the real thing. It is also built so that it can exactly simulate a myriad of emergencies or combinations of emergencies so that students can make mistakes and learn while safely on the ground.

Nevertheless, the primary purpose of the 2F137 is instrument flight training. It is programmed and instrumented to replicate actual flight. Mechanized so that it provides motion that mimics real climbs and turns, as well as the buffeting gusts of turbulence and the jolts of a violent thunderstorm, "flight" in the 2F137 is as close to an actual sortie in the weather as possible. It is from inside these devices that the students will gain much of the foundation that will enable them to truly fly on instruments alone.

The instruction includes emergency procedure training, so each sortie requires that one or more malfunctions be introduced. For a very long time the U.S. Navy's attitude has been that nothing prepares an aviator for an emergency in instrument flying conditions quite like practicing for an emergency in instrument flying conditions.

Of course, the students were exposed to simulators during primary training, but flying the 2F137 is different, as is, of course, the airspeed associated with jet flight.

Takeoffs occur more quickly, checklists must be performed more expeditiously, and altitude transitions and turns must be anticipated sooner. The mental pressures that the higher airspeeds place on the students are tremendous. Neophyte flyers were able to get through the earlier phase with a "150-knot mind," but the T-45 demands much more.

Although they respect and value what the 2F137 does for them, it does not take long for many of the students to develop a special dislike for the simulator. Just as they come to master one aspect of flight, another is introduced, and then another, until dealing with the most challenging dilemma from the week before becomes second nature while newly presented problems are nearly overwhelming. Because the simulators are so realistic and because the events demand so much focus and concentration, it is almost easy to forget that a simulated set of emergencies in foul weather with low fuel is not the real thing. There never has been a T-45 student who has not emerged from the instrument trainer at one time or another drenched with sweat, with hands still nervously shaking from a particularly grueling session. Still, it feels like energy well spent when the SNA has the first instrument flight in the actual aircraft (the real thing actually seems to fly easier and better than the simulator).

But the simulator's usefulness is not confined to emergency procedures or instrument flying. The 2F137's sibling, the 2F138, is put to good use for familiarization flying. Identical to the 2F137 except with a visual projection out the forward quadrants, the 2F138 helps to develop the spatial skills that the students will need to master flight in the real aircraft. Again, although this expertise can be taught using the actual T-45, the simulator helps to teach it at much less cost. The more mundane aspects of flight operations such as engine start, post-start checks, taxi, takeoff, basic aircraft handling and maneuvers, and landing can all be efficiently reviewed and practiced in the simulator.

Nevertheless, the nation's enemies are not going to be defeated by simulators, and the day finally arrives when the student is scheduled for his first familiarization sortie in the real aircraft. We'll call today's student "Bill." By now, Bill has completed seven familiarization simulator sorties, five emergency procedures sessions, and a number of instrument flight simulator and aircraft events. All of these have been augmented by daily academic instruction and computer-assisted tutoring. The aircraft is beginning to become familiar to Bill, —although he has yet to fly it outside of the instrument syllabus.

It is an exciting event, but a long one. The actual flying portion of the mission is only a part of the entire exercise. Just as he did during the primary phase, Bill spends many hours studying and "chair flying" prior to every simulator or flight event. Before the briefing begins today, Bill notes the forecast weather for the area, and double-checks that he can recite and answer the questions of the day (QODs) on the squadron's flight schedule. Then he studies even

A T-45 instructor emphasizes a briefing point with a model.

more while he waits in the squadron ready room. Bill is prepared for his flight and anxious for his instructor to call his name.

And then it happens. An instructor checks the schedule, looks at the new faces, and calls for Bill. After a short introduction, the two move to a briefing room and the event begins. Usually the briefing starts with a review of the QODs. It is during this beginning that the tone of the coming flight is set: the instructor carefully observes the quality of Bill's responses and the depth of his knowledge, as well as his manner and attitude. The instructor notes all of this and measures it against what is typical for this stage of the syllabus.

After the preliminaries have been dealt with, the instructor reviews the sortie's learning objectives and discusses the execution of particular maneuvers. Bill recites procedures verbatim, while the instructor quizzes him on various aspects of the different exercises that will be introduced and practiced. The instructor also details techniques that Bill might find useful and informs him what the expectations for this event are. Finally, after Bill has had time to ask any last questions, the older pilot concludes the briefing. After updating the weather once more, the two check their aircraft assignment and their operating area and then make their way downstairs to the flight equipment shop.

As ordinary as the task is, getting suited up for the first few sorties in a reasonable amount of time is a challenge for every new student. Instructors usually finish long before their students. Typically the student, flushed and

"Okay, put it on and meet me in maintenance control in two minutes."

hurried and looking like a "soup sandwich," arrives in the maintenance area well after his instructor. The more experienced pilot expects this and gives Bill time to catch his breath while they both review the aircraft discrepancy book (ADB).

The ADB is a maintenance log that describes recent maintenance the aircraft has undergone. It also carries records of previous flights and lists discrepancies or "gripes" that may or may not affect the upcoming flight (e.g., an inoperative map light that may preclude certain types of night sorties but not affect a daytime familiarization flight). Information of this sort is important for the pilots to review and evaluate. The instructor signs for the aircraft after determining that it is acceptable for the sortie. For all intents and purposes, the instructor now "owns" the aircraft and is responsible for what happens to it until it is safely parked at the end of the sortie. Later, when the students start flying solo missions, they will take responsibility for the aircraft and sign the ADB themselves.

At the aircraft the instructor follows Bill through a preflight inspection, asking questions along the way. By now Bill's academic instruction, as well as several self-paced inspections on his own time have, prepared him for this event. When satisfied with the youngster's performance, the instructor will allow Bill to climb into the front cockpit for the first time.

Their shadow since they stepped onto the parking ramp has been the aircraft's plane captain (see the preceding chapter). Bill is reassured by the familiarity of the cockpit and its instrumentation and setup. Sure enough, the simulator is an exact replica of the actual aircraft—right down to the cant of the seat and the feel of the switches. Still, there is plenty that is different. First, he must strap into the ejection seat; this is something not regularly practiced in the simulators, and the tightness of the belts and harnesses constricts his movement. The mask clamped over Bill's face is pushing oxygen into his mouth

The "flight gear flamenco" is danced out before every sortie.

The amount of survival equipment packed into a naval aviator's survival vest is impressive.

75

Improvements in materials and fit have made wearing the oxygen mask more bearable, it still takes some getting used to for the new students.

and nose whether he wants it or not; it will take time to get accustomed to this. And the noise! The flight line is a busy place, and the whine of jet motors pierces the air. All around aircraft are coming and going; it is difficult to hear the plane captain as he wishes Bill good luck and steps down to finish preparing the aircraft for flight.

Twisting around in his seat, Bill gets a thumbs-up from the instructor and starts through his checklists. It is just like the simulator—except that it is different. As seemingly real as the 2F137 and 2F138 are, there is no substitute for the real thing. The instructor is ready for the instances when Bill becomes stymied, and helps him

through the start and post-start checks. Although the hand signals from the plane captain are unfamiliar and seem to frustrate Bill, the instructor knows it will not be long before these procedures will come almost automatically to the student.

Communications, of course, are much different from what Bill is accustomed to in the 2F137 and 2F138. Rather than a simulator instructor responding with make-believe calls on a clear channel, Bill must pay attention to a myriad of transmissions coming from controllers in the tower and from other jets located all over the airfield. At the same time he is forced to listen to his breathing

The flight line at NAS Kingsville as seen through the raised canopy of a T-45.

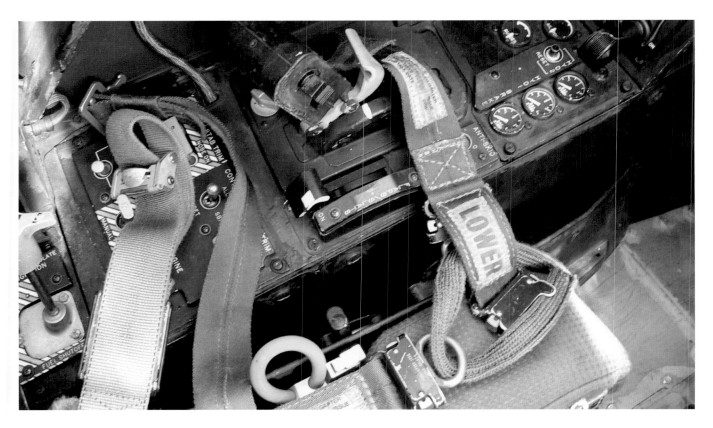

The cockpit of the T-45 can be intimidating initially. Leg restraints (one is marked "lower") keep legs from flailing in the event of an ejection. The small green loop handle activates emergency oxygen. The throttle has speedbrake and radio switches, and the flap lever is adjacent. The red-knobbed handle in the upper right raises and lowers the landing gear.

"And it's off-road capable too!" Actually, the taxiway that carries this T-45 is obscured by tall grass at NAS Kingsville.

over the intercom system as well as the prompts and suggestions the instructor expects him to respond to. It is confusing, and Bill must listen carefully to make his radio calls at the right moment. Equally important, he needs to be ready to listen and copy the instructions that come back to him.

Finally, checklists complete, Bill is ready to taxi. He is exhausted already and has not even made it to the runway! After checking his notes one last time he calls for clearance to taxi: "Ground, Two-Bravo-Two-Three-Zero, taxi one T-45 with information Charlie."

"Two-Bravo-Two-Three-Zero, Kingsville Ground, cleared to taxi to Runway 13 via Alpha and the parallel, follow Two-Bravo-Two-One-Six, the flight of four T-45s crossing in front of you from left to right. Altimeter is 29.99, contact tower in the hold short." Bill tries to digest what he has just been told while he checks the area around him and looks down at the waiting plane captain. Behind Bill his instructor calls, "Okay, you need to answer up—let's go."

It is going to be a long day.

Ten minutes later Bill has managed to taxi the aircraft out of the squadron's flight line and to the hold-short area at the end of the runway. He hopes that he will be able to remember the route during his next flight. After working his way through the takeoff checklist and making certain that everything is as it should be, he calls for takeoff clearance.

He receives it immediately.

Bill is like every other student who has gone through jet training; he feels as if he is well out of his element and hardly prepared to take the jet airborne. Breathing against the positive flow of the oxygen is difficult. His flight gear and the seat's harnesses seem to be working together to keep him from reaching anything in the cockpit without exerting too much effort. He is sweating underneath his helmet, and tasks that were simple in the simulator do not seem to make any sense in the aircraft. At this stage in the syllabus, though, Bill's confusion is expected, and the

The "B" on the vertical stabilizer of this T-45 marks it as a Training Air Wing TWO aircraft based at NAS Kingsville, Texas.

T-45A versus T-45C

Naval aviation's newer tactical strike aircraft have digital cockpits. The time is not too far away when all the aircraft that make up this community will have moved away from the traditional analog dials ("steam gauges"). The service is configuring its fleet of training aircraft to reflect the changes in the fleet. The T-6A II with its digital interfaces is part of this realignment.

Nevertheless, the first eighty or so T-45s, designated T-45As, were delivered with legacy-style instrumentation. These were sent to NAS Kingsville where they still serve. Modified aircraft, T-45Cs, were provided to the training units at NAS Meridian starting in December 1997. These aircraft are physically the same as the earlier jets, but with multifunction digital cockpit displays, improved avionics, and upgraded heads-up displays (HUDs). These are similar to the more advanced systems in the fleet, and serve to smooth the transition once the aviator is designated and leaves the training command. Bringing the T-45As up to T-45C standards has already begun, and plans call for all T-45s to be upgraded during the next several years.

A T-45 Goshawk lifts off as the pilot executes a touch-and-go at NAS Kingsville.

instructor coaxes him onto the runway. Once he aligns the jet with the centerline, Bill pushes the throttle forward and feels the engine spool up while he pushes hard against the brakes to keep the aircraft from leaping forward. Both he and his instructor check the cockpit gauges one more time, and after a last-minute wipeout of the controls, Bill releases the brakes and lets the aircraft roll.

In seconds the speedy little jet is racing down the runway. Bill works the rudder pedals to make small steering adjustments to keep the T-45 centered down the long stretch of pavement. In seemingly no time whatsoever, though, the aircraft rotates about its two main landing gear and lifts itself off the ground. Bill has just realized his childhood dream; he is flying a jet.

There is no time to savor the moment. The airspeed is building rapidly despite the fact that the aircraft is in a climb. Bill snaps up the landing gear handle only just in time to avoid breaking the placarded airspeed restrictions. Pushing through those important numbers might damage the aircraft. At the very least, an accidental excursion beyond the allowed airspeed will require maintenance action.

An instant after raising the landing gear, Bill brings the flaps up to keep the speed from damaging them as well. Now flying quickly away from the ground, Bill turns the aircraft on course and is surprised by its instantaneous response to even the smallest inputs. Headed in the right direction, he pulls the throttle back and pushes forward on the control stick—he has let his airspeed get out of control and is racing faster than the 250 knots he should be maintaining. He is also about to climb the T-45 through an altitude restriction. Over the ICS Bill hears the instructor chuckle. He tries not to get distracted and continues to point the bird toward their scheduled practice area. Flying jets is not easy.

But he is learning how. By the time Bill and the instructor arrive in their assigned airspace, he is already becoming accustomed to how the aircraft responds to his hands and feet. The simulator provides a very good replication of the actual aircraft, but it is not perfect, and Bill is discovering the differences now. While he grows more comfortable, the instructor directs him through a few turns and then takes control of the aircraft for a couple of minutes and demonstrates a basic stall. After the demonstration, the instructor passes the controls back to Bill, who tries to repeat the same maneuver. His first attempt is satisfactory and his second effort is good. The instructor offers up a few words of praise and takes the aircraft for a different demonstration. Again, Bill is able to fulfill the instructor's expectations with little difficulty.

Bill's confidence grows while the instructor and he practice the flight's required "high work." This early in the syllabus it is confined to simple turns and stalls. Later he

The equipment behind this T-45 makes up a TACAN, or Tactical Air Navigation, station.

By the time the typical student is midway through the T-45 syllabus the classes have gotten smaller and the attitude has grown more relaxed.

will be required to execute basic aerobatics and other more complex maneuvers. Soon, though, the mandated exercises for this sortie are complete, and Bill keys the radio to check out of the area and starts the jet back toward the airfield. Along the way he picks out local landmarks that were stressed during the course rules lectures. He'll need to be able to find his own way home in the event that a future solo flight finds him with failed navigation instruments. Weaving through scattered clouds, he notes how quickly they pass by his canopy: the speed difference between the T-45 and the T-34C he flew at Whiting Field is obvious now.

Close to the airfield the instructor takes control of the aircraft, descends, and enters the overhead traffic pattern with a hard, left-hand, five-g turn that has Bill seeing stars as the blood rushes out of his head and torso and into his legs despite the squeeze of the g-suit. After 180 degrees of turn, the instructor snaps the wings level and quickly calls out to Bill the criteria for setting the aircraft up for a good landing. After a quick review of the landing checklist, the instructor starts a gentle descending turn back toward the end of the runway. When the aircraft's wings are level

again, the T-45 is in a cocked-up attitude, at a precise airspeed, headed for an exact point on the pavement. Bill notes the Fresnel lens (an optical landing aid on the left edge of the runway that indicates if the aircraft is on the correct glideslope) and sees that the instructor has perfectly centered the "meatball" in the lens. He watches for just a bit more than fifteen seconds while the aircraft is expertly brought down for a perfect landing.

Following a quick touch-and-go, the instructor passes control of the aircraft to Bill, and Bill quickly turns downwind to set the aircraft up for landing. The pattern is crowded, and he not only has to keep an eye on the traffic around him while he flies the jet, but he also must monitor multiple radio calls as well as making his own transmissions at the appropriate time. It is not easy, and he soon forgets how well the high work went only a few minutes earlier. Bill peeks inside the cockpit at his instrument panel to double-check that his landing gear and flaps are down. When he looks up, he finds that his jet is angling toward the runway. After a quick turn to correct his heading, he hurries through the rest of the landing checklist. Now he is too far away from the runway. And too fast. And

This image captures a T-45 just at the instant of touchdown.

too low. Bill works the controls but forgets to make his radio call while he pulls power and starts a descent and turn at the same time. All the while his instructor covers his missed radio calls and coaches him through the procedures. The familiar sense of being overwhelmed returns to Bill.

By the time he points the aircraft toward the runway and rolls the wings level, Bill feels that he has forgotten almost everything he ever learned. Nevertheless, he works to control the speed and rate of descent of the jet. Several times he catches a fleeting glimpse of the meatball as it

races up or down the Fresnel lens, but his primary concern is a safe landing rather than a perfect one.

After Bill's first attempt at an acceptable touchdown, the instructor takes the controls again and demonstrates another. The two flyers make several more turns around the landing pattern, and Bill gradually starts to recognize mistakes and make corrections on his own. The meatball is actually somewhere on the lens during his last couple of passes. Finally, after nearly an hour and a half, the instructor takes the controls one last time and executes a full-stop landing.

A T-45 taxis into a crowded flightline.

Back on the ground, Bill completes the post-landing checklists and taxis the aircraft back to the flight line. There, a plane captain guides him into position and waits until he shuts the aircraft down. With a sharp snap of the wrist, Bill brings the throttle back, and the engine slowly whines itself down until it stops completely. He looks up and sees that his instructor has already climbed out of the jet. Feeling awkward, Bill disconnects himself from the radio and the oxygen hose, as well as the seat; he forgets the hose to the g-suit and it snaps out of its fitting when he stands up. After a moment or so of fumbling, he finally is able to crawl down to the parking ramp.

Following a quick stop through the maintenance spaces to fill out their paperwork, Bill and his instructor shuck their flight gear and make their way to a debriefing room. There, the instructor carefully reviews the flight and critiques every aspect of Bill's performance. Bill is surprised when his mentor compliments him on his preparation and attitude. She feels that it helped Bill perform better than average both at altitude and in the landing pattern. She encourages him to keep studying and reminds him not to let up on the chair flying.

After debriefing, despite his exhaustion, Bill feels a sense of accomplishment. But there is no time to relish his success. The briefing for his second flight on this day starts in less than an hour.

While they mark their way through the familiarization stage, the students also progress through the instrument

One of the perks of flying the T-45 is that the students get to "take a jet on the road" during their instrument training. Just returned, this student and instructor remove their bags from the pod slung underneath the aircraft.

flight syllabus. It is these flights that are most accurately simulated by the 2F137 devices, although the workload of the actual flight is arguably less because there is no good way to realistically conjure up most emergencies in the real aircraft. Rather, the students gain more valuable experience in the air while honing their blind-flying skills. To make the sorties as authentic as possible, though, the students are required to fly under a covering in the rear cockpit that denies them an outside visual reference. This exercise is derisively known as flying "under the bag" but it is an effective tool. One technique that instructors use to build students confidence is to take control of the aircraft just after the latter have finished an instrument approach. At that point the instructors allow the students to look out from under the bag so that they can see just how precisely the instruments—combined with their own newly learned skills—have lined the aircraft up for landing.

While initial sorties are confined to nearby training areas and local military airfields, it is not long before the students begin to range farther out into the national airspace and practice what they have learned during their basic instruction. Under close supervision they venture out into the high-altitude airways and mix with large commercial airliners as well as smaller, general civilian airplanes. This is the real-world classroom that teaches them how to deal with complex air traffic routing in difficult weather and crowded airspace. What initially seems to be almost impossibly difficult and bewildering beyond any hope of comprehension soon starts to make sense.

Note the excellent view from the rear cockpit of the T-45.

Opposite: The ejection seat is the only way to escape most tactical jet aircraft in flight—a traditional "bail out" is no longer an option. *USN/Mark Rebilas*

Ejection Seats

The first ejection seats used operationally were those of Hitler's Luftwaffe during World War II. The higher airspeeds of more advanced platforms were making it increasingly difficult to get out of a mortally stricken aircraft in the traditional manner of opening the canopy, unfastening the various restraints, climbing out of the cockpit, and safely jumping clear. The new seats were primitive affairs with hard-firing explosive charges that often failed, malfunctioned, and injured or even killed the pilots. Through the decades since they were introduced, the science and technology behind ejection seats has evolved to the point where the systems nearly always permit the pilot to safely get out of an aircraft from altitudes, attitudes, and airspeeds that would have once been a death sentence.

The T-45 is equipped with the naval aircrew common ejection seat (NACES). This is a complex but reliable system that can provide a safe ejection across a wide envelope of regimes—even from a plane stopped on the ground. Pilots with nude weights of from 100 to 235 pounds can expect a safe ejection if the attempt is made within prescribed limits. The students receive a thorough indoctrination about the seat, including detailed instruction on the functions of the many components and the various modes of operation.

Simply put, upon initiating the ejection with the single loop handle located between the flier's legs, two rocket motors ignite in sequence and send the seat up the twin rails that normally help to hold it in the cockpit. At nearly the same time, restraints pull the pilot's legs against the seat to prevent flailing injuries. An instant later the mild detonating cord (MDC) at the top of the canopy explodes and shatters the canopy to clear the way for the seat and its occupant. (In the event the MDC fails to function, hard points called "canopy breakers" at the top of the seat will smash through the canopy.) Once the seat clears the aircraft, a small drogue parachute deploys that in turn pulls out the main parachute. Later the seat separates itself from the pilot, leaving the pilot with the parachute and a seat pan equipped with a life raft and an assortment of survival equipment. The pilot then descends below the twenty-two-foot-diameter main parachute at approximately, twenty-two feet per second.

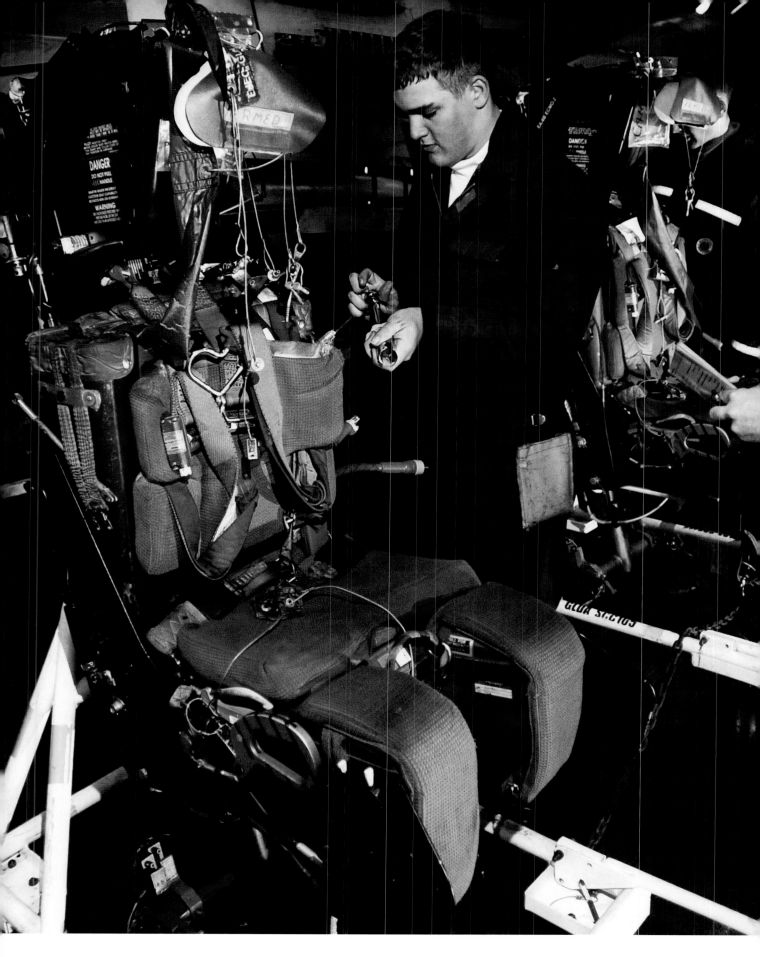

FIVE

An SH-60 Seahawk fires a Penguin antiship missile. *USN/Lisa Aman*

Rotary-Wing Aircraft

Today students practice air taxiing down a training squadron flight line on a bluebird day ashore.

Most of the young officers selected for helicopter training only need to change their commute very slightly. Not only does the U.S. Navy conduct most of its primary pilot training at NAS Whiting Field, it conducts its helicopter training there as well. The installation is actually made up of two airfields; primary training is done with the T-34Cs at the north airfield, and the south airfield is lined with long rows of orange and white Bell TH-57 Sea Ranger helicopters. Even those officers who had their initial flight training at NAS Corpus Christi or at one of the air force bases will find the area familiar. It is only about a forty-five–minute drive east of NAS Pensacola, where they all attended API together just a few months earlier.

As much as the students learn to be careful on the T-34C flight line, the TH-57 can be even more dangerous; it has a large rotor main rotor and a second tail rotor positioned exactly at face level.

means by which the pilot maintains altitude with a helicopter. Pulling up on the collective increases the pitch of the rotor blades and provides more lift, while pushing down on the collective decreases rotor blade pitch, thereby producing less lift. Because of the changing power demands on the engine that result from operation of the collective, there are various mechanical and electronic elements built into the system to ensure smooth operation.

At the top of the collective is the throttle or twist grip. It controls engine revolutions per minute (RPM) and operates similarly to a motorcycle throttle. Twisting the

throttle away from the pilot increases the RPM, while rotating it toward the pilot decreases RPM. Normally the twist grip is maintained in the fully open position. As the collective changes the pitch of the main rotor blades, and more or less power is required, a governor adjusts fuel flow to the engine to maintain constant RPM.

The antitorque pedals closely resemble the rudder pedals of a fixed-wing aircraft. Like rudder pedals, they are located on the floor of the cockpit and are operated by the feet to control movement of the aircraft around the vertical, or yaw, axis. However, antitorque pedals control

A lineup of TH-57 tails at NAS Whiting Field. Note the protective skids that curve out from each aircraft. These will help to protect the aircraft and the crew in the event that the students' flying gets out of parameters.

this movement by changing the pitch of the blades in the small tail rotor. Changes to the main rotor with resultant changes to the helicopter's airspeed and attitude create differences in torque that would render the aircraft uncontrollable without the tail rotor. Therefore, whenever there is a change in the collective there must be a coordinated application of yaw control via the antitorque pedals because, otherwise, there would be no way to maintain the helicopter's heading and balanced flight.

Of course, the preceding descriptions are gross simplifications of subject matter that takes weeks of study for the average SNAs to comprehend at a level that will meet the exacting standards of their instructors. The academic instruction and the various learning aids that are available help to ease the task. Nevertheless—just as during the primary phase—it is the students' own motivation and work ethic that ultimately carry the day. The complexities of rotary-winged flight are many and varied, and throughout their career the helicopter pilots will continue to refine and build upon the basics learned at NAS Whiting Field.

This student is carefully inspecting the tail rotor, which counteracts the torque caused by the larger main rotor.

The main rotor is obviously important to helicopter flight; its complicated system warrants careful inspection before flight.

SNAs are expected to spend a great deal of time in and around the aircraft before their first flight. Since the TH-57 is not only a new airframe for them, but also a completely new type of aircraft, it is important that the students become intimately familiar with its components and the functions and makeup of those components. Many of the gauges and instruments in the TH-57's cockpit are familiar, but there are also many controls and devices that are completely new, including the collective, the cyclic, and the twist grip. Aircraft are made available on the flight line for the students to practice their preflight inspections as well as their cockpit procedures. By the time of their first cockpit procedures trainer event, the SNAs have spent quite a bit of their own time becoming comfortable with the aircraft.

The TH-57 is a variant of the extremely popular and widely produced Bell 206 Jet Ranger, arguably the most successful commercial helicopter ever built. The Army's OH-58 Kiowa armed reconnaissance helicopter—first put into service during the Vietnam War—is perhaps the most recognized military version of the Jet Ranger series. Taking a cue from the Army's exhaustive evaluations, and noting the type's simplicity, economy of operation,

and reliability, the U.S. Navy selected it for service in the training role and took delivery of its first TH-57A in October 1968. The 40 original TH-57As accumulated many thousands of hours each before being replaced by 119 more modern TH-57B and TH-57C aircraft. These are the models still in service today. The TH-57C has a more advanced instrumentation suite than the TH-57B and is used for the later stages of the syllabus.

The aircraft has good flight characteristics similar to those of many of the helicopter types operated by the fleet.

The pilot has just lifted this TH-57 clear of the ramp and is preparing to air taxi.

The instrumentation in the TH-57's cockpit does not look particularly different or unusual when compared to the T-34C that most students train on.

The U.S. Navy uses its remaining CH-46Ds mainly for utility purposes. *USN/Nicole Carter*

It is also relatively easy to fly. Its cockpit arrangement allows for good interaction among the crew members and provides good visibility. The cabin has ample room for a second student who is used as an observer during instrument training. Often the two students will change places ("hot seating") and the crew will continue for a second flight.

The Rolls Royce (Allison) 250-C20BJ turbofan engine allows the aircraft to cruise at about 100 knots and gives it a top speed of more than 120 knots. The engine has

demonstrated the ability to take the aircraft up to 19,000 feet, though normal operating altitudes are much lower. Maximum range is more than 300 nautical miles. The airframe is of moderate size, with its rotors spanning a diameter in excess of 33 feet and a fuselage length just more than 39 feet. Its maximum gross weight is 3,200 pounds.

Every helicopter type in naval aviation is flown by a crew rather than by a single pilot. A crew has more resources—more eyes, brains, collective knowledge, and

The twin barrels of this AH-1W's 20mm cannon are clearly visible. TH-57 students will not receive any weapons training until they reach the fleet.
USN/Kyle Voigt

experience—and the U.S. Navy seeks to capitalize on these to increase the mission effectiveness and safety of its aircraft and crews. It has formalized this process through a concept called crew resource management. It is true that the SNAs receive some training and exposure to the concept during the primary phase, but it is emphasized even more in the helicopter pipeline. The Navy has classified the many skills and behaviors that influence CRM into seven basic areas: decision making, assertiveness, mission analysis, communication, leadership, adaptability/flexibility, and situational awareness. These seven basic areas are further broken down into many different subsets. Every aspect of a mission's execution will fall under one or more of these areas, and the exercise of good CRM—often nothing more than plain common sense—will take advantage of the strengths of the crew to help ensure that the mission is performed effectively and safely.

The first few flights are when students learn what is known as "low work," the maneuvers that take place close to the ground, and that must be mastered to execute the most basic procedures, which include the vertical takeoff, the hover, the turn on the spot, hover taxi, air taxi, and the vertical landing. All require finesse, concentration, and practice. The TH-57 Contact FTI emphasizes this:

> *Use pressures and small (very small) movements of the controls to maintain attitude, heading, and altitude. The key with helicopters is small precise application of pressures and movements as necessary. Position over the ground is maintained by making fine attitude changes, not by gross control movements put in and taken out. These large inputs usually only rock the helicopter and upset the passengers (and your instructor!).*

The novices' first attempt to lift off and hover a helicopter has been described as akin to "trying to play the piano while standing on top of a greased football that's perched on the back of a rodeo bull—with someone yelling at you." The experience is truly foreign and a bit frightening; it is nothing like flying the T-34C. A beginner is easy to spot on the ramp and in the practice area; the TH-57 lurches and wobbles like a toddler taking its first steps and would likely clatter out of control and into the ground if not for the steadying hands and feet of the instructor.

The task is made even more difficult by the nature of the environment. Even before their first flight, the students

are taught that the mass of air above the earth is very much a dynamic entity; it is in constant motion and moves both laterally and vertically. Like a body of water, it has currents as well as pockets of calm. Students encountered this to some extent in the primary syllabus, where they learned to counter the effects of wind in the landing pattern and make navigational corrections at altitude where the effects of winds were discernible but not immediately dangerous.

The five-seat TH-57 provides primary and advanced flight training for student aviators. (Note the tailmarking: "Marines.")

But the impact of winds is readily apparent during the low-work portion of the curriculum. The instant the helicopter becomes airborne it is subject to the same forces that send leaves or errant pieces of trash skittering across the ramp. A fifteen-knot gust at liftoff is actually a giant, invisible hand that, if not dealt with immediately, can send a helicopter careening out of its hover straight into another aircraft. The instructors' task is made all the more difficult by this additional factor, and the frustrations the students feel are palpable.

Nevertheless, enough practice can improve even the most incompetent early efforts. Although the initial sorties demand a great deal of patience and effort from the instructors, it does not take too many flights before the students begin to master their low work. Soon they are able to competently lift off from the parking spot, hover

This TH-57 is being air taxied just a few feet above the ramp. The photograph highlights the excellent visibility from the cockpit.

The second student, visible here in the cabin of the aircraft, acts as an observer. He is responsible for watching for other aircraft or anything else that may endanger the helicopter.

taxi forward, execute a turn on the spot, and taxi clear of the parking ramp.

Square patterns are exercises that help the trainees practice and refine low work. There are three types of square patterns: perpendicular, parallel, and constant heading. When flying the perpendicular-heading square, students slide the aircraft around the outside edges of a marked square with the nose of the aircraft perpendicular to each side, pointing toward the inside of the square.

This requires reorientation, or changing the heading of the helicopter by ninety degrees as the trainees work their way around each corner. The parallel-heading square simply has the students following the trace of the square, with the fuselage of the helicopter parallel to the side of the square he is flying over. Again, they must change the heading at each corner. The constant-heading square requires the novices to trace the edges of the square while maintaining a constant heading. No turns are required at the corners,

This is one of the most demanding missions a CH-53E pilot—or any pilot—can fly. *USMC/Paula Fitzgerald*

but rather the students must slide left or right, or hover taxi forward or aft depending on their position over the edges of the square.

Common mistakes for all the patterns include rushing the maneuver, getting fixated on the square rather than maintaining a constantly sweeping scan, failing to correct for or anticipate the effects of wind, lack of precision when negotiating corners, and failing to maintain a constant altitude. Nevertheless, the exercises are very effective at teaching the new fliers the nuances of control and precision. The instructors can tell the SNAs how to use gentle control pressures and how to anticipate what the aircraft is going to do next, but the pupils must experience it all themselves.

During this stage the students also acquire the skills to perform the types of basic maneuvers that must become intuitive for them to be effective naval aviators. They learn how to execute a no-hover takeoff and how to make the transition to forward flight. Among many other maneuvers they learn how to execute maximum-load takeoffs, how to climb, how to switch to a level cruise profile, how to perform balanced turns, and how to execute descents and approaches to landings. Becoming expert at all of these exercises challenges the neophytes' motor skills and their ability to multitask. Not only are they expected to fly the required maneuvers—and fly them well—but they must also navigate and talk on the radios. Finally, they must be able to properly handle whatever simulated emergencies the instructor imposes.

One of the most frequently practiced emergencies, and the one that causes perhaps the greatest anxiety, is the autorotation. This is the maneuver that enables the crew to execute a safe landing in the event of an engine failure. The TH-57 FTI says that the autorotation is "a condition of non-powered flight in which the rotor speed and lift result from the reversed airflow through the rotor system." The student learns several ways to conduct different types of autorotations, each appropriate for a specific situation. Simply explained, what occurs during engine failure (actual or simulated) is that the pilot adjusts the attitude and rate of descent of the helicopter while determining where to land. The descent is steeper than normal, and the collective is lowered to reduce the pitch of the rotor blades. This in turn causes them to rotate faster, in essence building up energy. During the descent the pilot completes the checklists, picks a spot to land, maintains balanced flight, and judiciously manages the energy being created by the flow

The camera makes these helicopters appear closer than they actually are, but still the pilots must be exceedingly careful when moving around other aircraft

of air through the rotor system. Then, just before impact with the ground, the pilot has one opportunity to take advantage of the energy created. The pilot raises the collective, thus increasing the pitch of the blades and slowing the descent of the helicopter. At the same time the pilots uses coordinated cyclic and antitorque pedal inputs to make a balanced and cushioned landing.

Initially autorotation is a daunting maneuver, but with practice comes proficiency, and soon autorotation becomes something of a thrill, a carnival ride on Uncle Sam's dime. The FTI alludes to this somewhat:

Under most conditions it is easy to make a smooth touchdown from an autorotation in the TH-57. The trouble is there are still a few ways to foul it up; tension, inexperience and ignorance are at the root of most difficulties. Learn all you can about this maneuver and develop a feel for all the variables involved. With knowledge and proficiency comes confidence, and confidence relieves tension. This can be the most enjoyable maneuver you will do!

If all goes well, the SNA will qualify for solo flight after approximately fifteen flights and twenty-five hours of flight time. Solo flight is a bit of a misnomer; as students are actually paired with other pupils who are at roughly the same stage of instruction. This is not unrealistic, for there are no Navy, Marine, or Coast Guard helicopters not flown by a crew; in other words, there is no solo flight in Navy rotary-wing aviation. Together, the two students have a briefing with an instructor, and then with each other, before signing for an aircraft and flying it. Important considerations for these flights are the division of duties as delineated by NATOPS, squadron standard operating procedures, and the preflight brief. The flights themselves are almost always uneventful and validate the quality of the SNAs' training.

Another important portion of this stage of the curriculum is night flight. Because helicopter flight takes place in three dimensions and often quite close to the ground, it is important that the pilots be aware of all the factors that can affect their ability to control aircraft at night. Two of the most important are the decrease of depth perception and the loss or degradation of visual cues; these make the pilot more susceptible to vertigo and other disorienting phenomena. Because it is more difficult to see at night, whether inside the cockpit or out, students are taught to plan extra time for normally simple procedures like preflight and checklists. The instruction that students receive over a series of flights will help them successfully adapt to the peculiarities and vagaries of night flying.

Instead of the navigation at higher altitudes that the SNAs became familiar with during the primary syllabus, they now learn how to make their way from one location to another while operating as low as 200 feet above ground level and at speeds as high as 100 knots. The science of using time, distance, and heading plotted against preplanned routes on a chart is taught and underscored in the classroom and then practiced in the aircraft.

Reaching an acceptable level of competence is more difficult than it would seem. The simple act of fixing a position on a chart while moving across the ground at 100 knots is difficult enough without also having to keep the aircraft heading in the right direction, staying clear of the ground and other obstacles, and communicating on the radio. On the chart there is little to distinguish one road from another, most towns look the same, and the squiggly blue lines that mark streams or rivers often bear little resemblance to the actual waterways. As with everything in aviation, though, practice improves the proficiency of the fledgling fliers, and their performance improves with instruction and experience.

Advanced navigation aids—especially GPS—are becoming more prevalent, and the TH-57C is equipped with a very extensive navigational suite. The extreme accuracy inherent in GPS equipment can mitigate many of the problems associated with low-level navigation, and it is during this phase that its operation is introduced in the tactical role. Its value becomes immediately apparent to the students. Nevertheless, the basic skills associated with navigating by chart and compass are heavily stressed and graded; they are essentials that must be mastered in the event that equipment failure or enemy action precludes the use of GPS equipment.

Just getting from one point to another does little good unless the crew members can execute their mission once they arrive. This often requires landing and taking off in difficult or hostile terrain. The students are taught various approach, landing, and takeoff procedures and techniques that serve as basics for later training.

In combat, weather favors those who can operate in it, and our nation demands that its naval aviators be able to carry out their missions every hour of every day in all sorts of environmental conditions. The rotary-wing syllabus provides this training: upon completion of the curriculum the students will be fully instrument rated.

Basic instrument instruction teaches the SNAs how to develop a good visual scan across the various instruments and indicators that help them to maintain control of the aircraft through a variety of maneuvers. First in the simulator and later in the TH-57, the students become comfortable with blind-flying and keeping the aircraft appropriately trimmed for a given regime of flight, be it a climb, a descent, a turn, or level flight. Various turning and climbing patterns are practiced until enough proficiency is demonstrated so that turns and climbs together in the same exercise can be introduced and mastered. Flight on partial instrumentation is practiced as well. The student even learns how to execute an autorotation in poor weather conditions; engine failures do not occur only on clear days.

Radio instrument training builds on basic instrument skills to teach the SNAs how to fly actual instrument procedures (i.e., departures and arrivals from airfields). They become expert at flying approaches using TACAN (tactical air navigation), VOR (very high frequency

omni- directional radio) and NDB (nondirectional beacon) equipment. This sort of flying also makes best use of one of the benefits of a two-man crew, as an extra crew member takes on some of the workload and provides checks and balances that do no exist in aircraft with a single pilot.

By the time the fledgling helicopter pilots have completed the instrument phase of training at NAS Whiting Field, they have mastered the basics of all-weather flying as well as the more complex intricacies of instrument approaches and terminal procedures. They are expert at navigating from point-to-point and are eminently comfortable with flying in the national airspace with other military and civilian aircraft.

Although precision flying in all weather conditions has never brought the enemy to his knees, the ability to fly in near-zero visibility during horrid weather conditions allows naval aviators to apply tactical force when and where it is required. Even though the nation's foes are mostly far from the average students' thoughts when they have their noses buried in the books, those foes are the reason for the training. So, following the instrument stage, the students are introduced to aspects of flight that relate more directly to assignment to the fleet. This instruction includes tactical-flight maneuvers, confined-area landings, external-load operations, pinnacle landings, search-and-rescue procedures, shipboard operations, formation flight, use of night-vision devices, and section low-level navigation. The FTI for this final phase describes these tactically oriented operations as "the capstone of this stage." The proficiencies learned here will round out the skills that the newly fledged aviators will take to the fleet.

The initial portions of this instruction teach the SNAs how to approach and enter a landing zone in the quickest manner while minimizing risks from enemy actions. Students are taught how to choose and execute an approach and landing while taking into account the terrain, the size of the landing zone, environmental considerations (e.g., wind, sun, visibility), enemy fields of fire, aircraft weight, and power available. In addition, techniques are taught for confined-area operations and how to coordinate with the rest of the crew to ensure a successful maneuver. Being able to set down on the crowded deck of a ship, a cluttered urban parking lot, or a small jungle clearing can mean the difference between life and death, mission success and mission failure.

Initially, the controls for the TH-57 are baffling to the new students.

The TH-57 helps train students for assignment to the MV-22 Osprey. *USN*

Young helicopter pilots learn that time is the most critical factor in conducting search-and rescue (SAR) operations. Time is influenced by several factors, three of which are hours of daylight available, the degree of exposure to the elements that the survivor or survivors can stand, and the amount of time for SAR operations that the fuel on board the search aircraft allows. Hurried preparations and sloppy execution are the enemies of good SAR pro-

cedures, and so the students are taught a balance between the need to expedite and the need to plan.

Search patterns are an important aspect of SAR operations, and the SNAs are taught which is best for a given situation. The parallel pattern is used for a large search area when only the approximate initial position is known, whereas a creeping line pattern is used when the survivor is thought to be somewhere on a line between two points

Some TH-57 students will go on to fly the Marine Corps' CH-53E or the U.S. Navy's MH-53E variant. *USMC/Michael Gonzalez*

and probably closer to one point than another. A square pattern is used to search a small area when there is uncertainty about the initial position of the survivor, and a sector search is used when the reported position of the survivor is thought to be reliable. The young pilots also learn to take into account currents, sea conditions, visibility, and the enemy situation, among others. They are also taught to use their onboard gear as well as the equipment of other platforms in the area in order to enhance their efforts. Finally, they are taught the best types of approaches, given varying conditions, for executing the rescue when the survivor is finally located.

Navy and Marine helicopter pilots land on Navy ships. There are Navy instructions much longer and more detailed than this book that outline exact procedures and techniques for shipboard operations. The students spend

Aside from search and-rescue missions and security operations, the U.S. Coast Guard uses its HH-60 Jayhawk for boarding and searching suspicious ships. *USCG/Dave Hardesty*

a great deal of time becoming familiar with these documents and learning the essentials of how to safely and efficiently bring a helicopter aboard a ship in all sorts of weather. Not only do they need to factor in the environment and how it affects their aircraft, but they must also consider the ship and how it is being affected. As the pilots advance to the fleet, they will learn how to apply their instrument training to conduct approaches in both clear and foul weather, and they will learn the peculiarities of each type of ship from which they will operate.

Ultimately, after practicing over dry land, the students fly just off the coast to apply what they have learned on the real thing—the helicopter landing trainer (IX-514).

This small vessel is specially operated just for the purpose of familiarizing the new helicopter pilots with shipboard operations. It has a small landing deck, light signals, navigational equipment, and deck personnel, just as operational ships do. The same principles and procedures that apply in the fleet are exercised here, although the SNAs will get much more extensive training once they receive their wings and work with an operational aircraft type. The exercise itself, although somewhat of a "training wheels" event, is exciting and rewarding, and gives new helicopter pilots a taste of what to expect later on.

In the tactical environment, particularly during combat, helicopters almost always operate in formations

Opposite: The SH-3 Sea King is an aged warrior whose time in U.S. Navy service is nearing an end. Here, a special boat unit practices a medevac drill with an SH-3 based in San Diego. *USN/Katrina Beeler*

Medal of Honor Winner Stephen W. Pless

Heroism is found in all manner of cockpits. Some of naval aviation's finest hours were created by men who flew helicopters. Below is the citation for the Medal of Honor that was awarded to the pilot of a U.S. Marine Corps UH-1E in Vietnam, Stephen W. Pless:

For conspicuous gallantry and intrepidity at the risk of his life above and beyond the call of duty while serving as a helicopter gunship pilot attached to Marine Observation Squadron Six in action against enemy forces near Quang Ngai, Republic of Vietnam, on 19 August 1967. During an escort mission Major (then Captain) Pless monitored an emergency call that four American soldiers stranded on a nearby beach, were being overwhelmed by a large Viet Cong force. Major Pless flew to the scene and found 30 to 50 enemy soldiers in the open [at coords BS 743 782]. Some of the enemy were bayoneting and beating the downed Americans. Major Pless displayed exceptional airmanship as he launched a devastating attack against the enemy force, killing or wounding many of the enemy and driving the remainder back into a treeline. His rocket and machine gun attacks were made at such low levels that the aircraft flew through debris created by explosions from its rockets. Seeing one of the wounded soldiers gesture for assistance, he maneuvered his helicopter into a position between the wounded men and the enemy, providing a shield which permitted his crew to retrieve the wounded. During the rescue the enemy directed intense fire at the helicopter and rushed the aircraft again and again, closing to within a few feet before being beaten back. When the wounded men were aboard, Major Pless maneuvered the helicopter out to sea. Before it became safely airborne, the overloaded aircraft settled four times into the water. Displaying superb airmanship, he finally got the helicopter aloft. Major Pless' extraordinary heroism coupled with his outstanding flying skill prevented the annihilation of the tiny force. His courageous actions reflect great credit upon himself and uphold the highest traditions of the Marine Corps and the United States Naval Service.

—For their bravery, the rest of Pless's crew was awarded the Navy Cross.

From left to right, Lance Corporal John Phelps, Major Stephen Pless, Captain Rupert Fairfield, and Gunnery Sergeant Leroy Poulson. This Marine Corps helicopter crew was the most decorated in U.S. history, having earned one Medal of Honor and three Navy Crosses between them for their gallantry in Vietnam on August 19, 1967. *USMC*

External lift is an important mission for nearly all U.S. Navy helicopter types. Students learn the fundamentals of this mission while flying the TH-57. *USN*

of two or more aircraft. This is done for such reasons as mutual protection, concentration of firepower, and getting more aircraft more quickly to a given point. Formation flying comes to a fleet aviator nearly as naturally as breathing, but it is only grasped after much practice.

This type of aviation is described by the FTI:

> *Essentially, formation flying is nothing more than controlling the relative motion between aircraft. To maintain a fixed position the relative motion must be stopped. To maneuver safely in relation to another aircraft, the direction and rate of motion are controlled. Lead is considered "fixed" and any movement between aircraft is considered as movement of Wing in relation to Lead. In formation flying, Lead becomes the primary reference.*

Although formation flight was taught to the neophyte fliers during primary training, those lessons covered just the barest essentials. During the helicopter phase the students are exposed to all manner of formation flight and given the tools and experience that they will further build upon when they reach the fleet. The youngsters are taught how to maintain close ("parade") formation. This type of flying

HMX-1 is the Marine Corps helicopter squadron charged with providing helicopter transportation for the U.S. president and other dignitaries. *USMC*

The U.S. Coast Guard HH-65 Dolphin is a French design that flies many types of missions. It is a beautiful craft but has been criticized for poor reliability as well as limited payload and range. *USCG/Tom Sperduto*

puts two helicopters as close together as allowable and is useful for maintaining sight of each other while penetrating clouds or fog. This type of flying demands that the helicopter's controls be moved not by measured, mechanical inputs from the pilots, but almost as barely perceptible nuances or hints of movement. The wingman maintains position on the lead aircraft by moving the ship in increments of only a foot or so at a time. Also, the lead pilot must ensure that he moves his aircraft in an easy and predictable fashion. Abrupt or erratic control can cause a collision that will end in disaster.

Cruise formation has the aircraft flying a little farther apart, and allows the lead pilot to maneuver the helicopter more aggressively as may be required to avoid terrain, obstacles, other aircraft, or enemy fire. It is also the formation most often used in clear weather when there is no real threat of the pilots losing sight of each other due to fog or clouds. This type of flying is less stressful and allows the crews to relax a bit more than they would be able to do if they were maintaining a parade profile.

The SNAs learn to fly approaches to landings while in formation as well as all manner of takeoffs. They learn how to break formation as well as to rejoin, and they practice changing positions and roles while in flight. And importantly, they learn to navigate across terrain at low altitude while joined together. Through this phase they begin to appreciate the different roles played—the wingman performs the difficult chore of maintaining a perfect position relative to the lead, but the lead pilot must think ahead and plan for two or more aircraft, for the lead is ultimately responsible for the success of the aircraft that make up the formation.

One of the last stages of the helicopter syllabus is night flight with the aid of night vision goggles (NVGs). To take advantage of the cover of darkness, U.S. forces have striven increasingly to conduct a great deal of their combat operations at night. This has yielded great benefits because our nation's enemies typically lack the equipment and training to effectively fight in the dark. Chief among the tools that enable this night-fighting capability are NVGs. The device that the students train

Two TH-57s fly over the beach not far from Pensacola. Their broad rotor arcs keep them from flying as closely together as fixed-wing aircraft. The blue water and white, sandy beaches are tempting distractions to students as they work their way through training. *USN/Tom Thomas*

with, the AN/AVS-9, collects ambient light and passes it through an array of lenses and tubes to amplify the existing low levels of light from the moon, stars, or manmade lighting (e.g., urban locations).

The effectiveness of the device is startling to novices when they first put it on. The pitch black of night is converted to a shadowy, monochromatic green world that, while far from crystal clear, is more than adequate to accomplish nearly everything that can be performed during daylight. Nighttime tasks that previously would have seemed difficult to impossible are now seemingly simple.

NVGs are not perfect, and in fact pose a certain amount of danger if the aircrew members are not aware of the limitations and potential pitfalls associated with their use. First, the acuity provided by the devices is not great enough to allow the completion of tasks that require fine vision. While lighted objects can be seen from very far away, unlighted ones are more difficult to spot. The field of vision—only about forty degrees—is vastly inferior to the unaided eye's normal field of vision of approximately 180 degrees. Simple visible cues such as contrast and texture are reduced; depth perception is also degraded, and in certain very low–light conditions there is not enough illumination for the goggles to be of any use at all. The devices themselves must be well main-

tained to operate at peak condition, and the pilot must be able to adjust, focus, and mount them correctly—not an easy task. And although they are not very heavy, their weight is enough to cause some eyestrain and fatigue after a time.

These shortcomings can combine to pose a danger to the crews if they are not properly trained to recognize them and compensate accordingly. There have been too many cases when accidents were caused by overconfidence brought on by the NVGs. (For example, crews have flown into the ground or into obstacles they did not see—as well as into each other. Skewed depth perception has contributed to landing accidents that would not have occurred otherwise; and "blooming" caused by sudden and unexpected flashes of light has caused temporary blindness.)

On average, the Advanced Helicopter MPTS is scheduled to take students six months to complete. Barring unusually poor weather this is fairly realistic. By the time the rotary-wing students have finished, they will have spent five periods of instruction in the CPT and flown 20 simulator flights for a total of about 40 hours. In the actual aircraft the students will have flown approximately 70 sorties for a total of nearly 120 flight hours. Successful completion of the course means that SNAs have joined an elite, being officially designated naval aviators and awarded the coveted Wings of Gold.

Preflight check of the T-44's starboard propeller. The warning behind these two pilots is for those approaching the aircraft; they need to be aware of the danger posed by the blades.

A student does a preflight check of the starboard aileron of a T-44.

Unlike the T-34C, the cockpit arrangement in the T-44 allows quite a bit of interaction between the student and the instructor.

The size of the TC-12B can be better appreciated from this vantage point. Its usefulness in its former life as a utility aircraft is more obvious but its passenger and cargo-carrying capacity is rarely put to use in the training command.

uncommon event, it occurs often enough that thorough training is essential. Few multi-engine aviators finish their first fleet tour without experiencing engine problems at least once. Not only will the new fliers practice flying on just one engine during the familiarization stage, but they will have to demonstrate the ability to master single-engine flight while flying in instrument conditions. This latter challenge at first seems insurmountable, but after hours of practice in both the simulator and the aircraft it becomes

almost second nature. Another maneuver introduced and practiced during this phase of training is "ditching," a crash-landing in the water. Of course, the students do not actually put the aircraft in the water, but practicing to do so in various sea states will increase the odds of survival in the unlikely event the aircraft is forced down away from shore.

The students become more familiar with the crew coordination concept—sharing duties with their instructors just as crews share tasks aboard P-3Cs and C-130s. It takes skill to fly an aircraft alone, but to completely capitalize on all the advantages a full crew can confer also takes a special talent that comes only after a great deal of preparation and practice that is officially known as crew resource management (CRM). This introduction to crew coordination exposes future aircraft commanders to the fundamentals to be used when charged with leading a much larger crew on considerably bigger and more complex aircraft.

As expert as the new pilots are expected to be at flying in instrument conditions or on one engine, the enemy is not found and defeated by an excellent instrument scan or a perfect single-engine landing. Rather, the missions the SNAs will execute once they reach their tactical squadrons may call for them to fly low over the water in atrocious weather while flying precise patterns to, for instance, pinpoint the position of an enemy submarine, exactly place a pattern of antishipping mines, or meet and refuel a strike group.

One of the U.S. Coast Guard's best search-and-rescue assets is the C-130. *USCG/Tom Gillespie*

The student piloting this T-44A is doing a nice job taxiing along the yellow lines. On a large airfield, simply navigating from one spot to another safely and as directed by ground control can be quite a challenge.

Students slated for assignment to the E-2C Hawkeye will receive multi-engine training at NAS Corpus Christi. *USN/Dustin Howell*

This T-44 is landing beyond the arresting gear at NAS Kingsville.

Nevertheless, "stick-and-rudder" expertise makes up only part of the skill set required to execute the maritime mission. Those talents are useless if pilots and crew are not trained well enough to get to the operating area and back to base. Accordingly, over-water navigation is stressed as part of the syllabus. The students learn to navigate by the rudimentary precepts of dead reckoning, which is one of the oldest methods of navigation and requires the pilot to hold a given heading and airspeed for a certain time. The SNAs also learn to keep their position with such modern equipment as GPS (a means of navigation that relies on a constellation of satellites that broadcast precise signals) that is becoming more commonplace and is extraordinarily accurate. It is far from fail-safe, however, so all naval aviators receive good, basic instruction that will serve them well in the event technology fails them.

A mission constantly exercised in the real world, particularly by U.S. Navy crews, calls for the detection and identification of maritime vessels. To do this, the crews must fly low enough and close enough to be able to visually make out the hull numbers or names of the ships that interest them. Dropping down low over the water in a combination of maneuvers known as "rigging," the crews position their aircraft so that they can capture the information they need. There are a number of different procedures for doing this, and the students are expected to learn several of them. Fortunately, the Gulf of Mexico is fairly well trafficked, and the students have little trouble finding vessels to serve as ad hoc "targets."

A P-3C Orion drops an aerial mine (actually a modified general-purpose, aircraft bomb). *USN/Joseph Krypel*

This E-2C has just come aboard with only a single engine operating. *USN/Daniel McLain*

The C-2 Greyhound is not the prettiest aircraft in the world—until it's loaded with mail from home or filled with important cargo. *USN/Kathleen Gorby*

Successful completion of the multi-engine course at NAS Corpus Christi will see the students "winged" and designated naval aviators. They will have flown an average of just more than 100 multi-engine flight hours in five to six months. The flights, in combination with approximately twenty simulator events and extensive classroom and self-paced instruction, prepare them for the rigors of follow-on instruction on their assigned fleet aircraft.

Although most of the students who train at NAS Corpus Christi following the primary phase are assigned to the advanced maritime pipeline which prepares them for follow-on training on the P-3C or C-130, there are two other, more specialized, training pipelines. One of the pipelines is the intermediate E-2/C-2 phase. This instruction prepares students for their ultimate assignments as pilots of either the E-2C Hawkeye airborne early warning aircraft, or the C-2A Greyhound carrier onboard delivery aircraft. Both are twin-engine turboprops; the E-2C is flown from carriers, while the C-2A makes regular sorties to the aircraft carriers to deliver parts, supplies, people, mail, and other necessities. Rather than receiving their wings after their multi-engine training, the students in this pipeline will go to NAS Meridian or NAS Kingsville for an abbreviated T-45 syllabus that will ready them for carrier qualification.

A special syllabus is designed to prepare Marine Corps students for assignment to the MV-22 Osprey. The unusual handling characteristics of tilt-rotor aircraft demand special preparation, and a tailored multi-engine phase of instruction is part of this effort. At present, the best method for learning to fly the Osprey is still being explored, and it is certain that the training syllabus will evolve further over time.

Two students often fly together with an instructor during multi-engine training. *USN/Rich Stewart*

The Raytheon T-1A Jayhawk is used by the U.S. Navy and the U.S. Air Force for training. *USAF*

Other Multi-Engine Training

There are aircraft types in the U.S. Navy and Marine Corps that do not quite fit in the neat category of multi-engine aircraft occupied by the P-3C and the C-130 and its variants. For instance, the E-2C Hawkeye and the C-2A Greyhound differ from their larger brethren because they operate from aircraft carriers. From a training standpoint this poses an additional set of requirements beyond what is taught in the standard multi-engine syllabus. Accordingly, a separate curriculum (E-2/C-2) has been developed to meet these needs. The students selected for E-2C and C-2A service are identified early and matriculate through a multi-engine syllabus at Corpus Christi. They then go on to NAS Kingsville to fly various portions of the T-45 curriculum. By the time that their training is complete, they have developed the skills required to train effectively on either the Hawkeye or the Greyhound.

Another unique case is the Marines Corps' (and eventually the Air Force's and Navy's) MV-22 Osprey tilt-rotor; it is a new type of aircraft that has no training counterpart. Currently, students slated for assignment to the MV-22 are flying modified rotary-wing and multi-engine syllabuses. There is no doubt that this training will continue to develop and change as more is learned about tilt-rotor operations and requirements.

The EP-3E Aries II has a mission that is largely classified but that includes electronic eavesdropping. USN/S. J. Xanos

The E-2D is just entering service, and includes many improvements over the E-2C. USN/Ryan O'Connor

127

The canopy on the T-45, which opens sideways is operated manually ("pilot power").

Formation flying is simply an accepted part of doing business in naval aviation—a skill that is developed and practiced to do a job. For instance, the crews of a section (i.e., a pair) of jets assigned to carry out a mission in poor weather may perform a formation takeoff, that is, lifting off side-by-side, and then tuck tightly together to climb through a thick layer of clouds without losing sight of each other. Once clear of the weather, the pilots might separate a bit from each other in order to relax and perform various weapons checks, but often will rejoin to rendezvous on an aerial refueler such as a Marine KC-130 or a Navy F/A-18E Super Hornet. Once they are formed on the tanker, the pilots fly themselves into a position just behind

and below the baskets attached to the hoses trailing from the refueling aircraft. At the same time they deploy their refueling probes and stabilize their jets. Once properly positioned, they close on the baskets at a differential speed of two or three knots, and gently glide their probes into the connection at the end of the refueling hose. The complete exercise is measured in inches.

After taking on their fuel, the pair proceeds with the mission. Once the tactical portion of the sortie is complete, they may very well take on more fuel again before recovering to their base. (There is a good chance that if the weather was poor during takeoff, it will be bad when the time comes to land. This may require the two ships to

The T-45 instructor's view from the rear cockpit.

The instructor watches that a student does not taxi too close to the aircraft in front: "Foreign Object Damage" can harm or destroy the engine. *USN/John Andress*

Two T-45 students practice flying close to each other, in "parade formation."

This T-45 student is flying a close parade formation. It takes practice to learn to relax when the reality is that a miscue can send both aircraft crashing to earth.

Mk-76 practice bombs mounted beneath the wings of this pair of T-45s look almost comical, but their ballistics represent those of the general-purpose series of high explosive bombs that range from 500 to 2,000 pounds.

During the later stages of their training the T-45 students are expected to take on more and more responsibility, including briefing and leading flights.

again form up just a few feet apart while the lead aircraft takes them down on an instrument approach and perhaps a formation landing.)

The skills required to operate in close proximity to other aircraft were introduced during primary flight training, but that initial exposure was just a preliminary sampler of the talent required to fly in the fleet. To be truly effective, pilots assigned to fly tactical jets must be able to control their aircraft so precisely that corrections in inches ultimately come with little or no conscious thought.

The T-45 student learns the roles that each pilot in a formation must take. The flight lead is accountable for the safe conduct of the flight, and for getting the formation to and from the area of operations. The lead is responsible for radio communications within the flight and with outside entities and also coordinates the handling of any emergencies should they arise during the course of the sortie. The wingman is responsible for maintaining the integrity of the flight—for staying in position and maintaining sight. Formation flight begins on the ground, and the student quickly learns how and where to marshal and how to taxi as a flight. There are also several different types of rendezvous after takeoff, and the student becomes proficient at exercising all of them. Before getting airborne on the first multi-plane flight, the SNA will be very familiar with the different hand signals, which are important because they allow the flight to communicate without

unnecessary radio chatter. They also convey information from aircraft to aircraft in the event of radio failure.

Once airborne, the SNAs refine what was learned during the primary phase of instruction. In parade, or close formation, straight-and-level flight is practiced, and the young flyers adapt to using specific points on the lead aircraft as references in order to properly position their own. At the same time, they learn to periodically

The target as it appears from the instructor's rear cockpit from about 1,000 feet and 400 knots.

Training ranges over southern California and in Arizona are among the most heavily trafficked in the world. Here an instructor watches for other aircraft while his student concentrates on flying good formation.

scan the other aircraft in its entirety to maintain perspective, depth perception, and situational awareness. Formation flight demands minute, continuous control and power inputs, and it quickly becomes apparent that every correction requires a countercorrection that in turn must be countered, and so on. Turns into and away from the wingman are introduced, and the basics of these two simple maneuvers must be quickly mastered. Splitting and rejoining the flight—or breakup and rendezvous practice—is drilled ad nauseam. That formation flight is really a three-dimensional exercise in vectors soon becomes apparent.

Because the entire concept is so novel, and so much happens so quickly, it is normal for the neophytes to become anxious and overwhelmed. Nevertheless, formation flight demands that the pilots be relaxed—something that seems absolutely counterintuitive. From the rear cockpit the instructors work to convey a sense of calm and composure and try to impart that same mindset to their students. One of the age-old tricks of the trade that instructors use when SNAs are tense and jerky and appear to be "killing snakes in the cockpit" is to urge them to

A wingman as viewed through the rear-view mirror mounted on the T-45's canopy bow.

"wiggle your toes." The effort to do so takes just enough mental effort that the students' over-wringing of the controls often eases and the aircraft oscillations smooth out accordingly.

Formation flying is not all about flying off of another aircraft. The lead pilot does not have to worry about maintaining position, but has other concerns. This pilot must think ahead of the flight to get the formation safely from one point to another. The lead does not have the luxury of aggressively turning the aircraft to get where the flight needs to go. Every maneuver and power change must be smooth and deliberate so that any wingman can match the lead aircraft's movement and stay in position. The lead pilot must adopt a mindset of care and consideration. Even at the controls of a nimble jet, the pilot must act and fly as if there are a dozen helpless, naked-pink babies balanced on the wings.

After a time the young pilots become more proficient and comfortable with flying very near to other aircraft. They are introduced to night formation flight and to cruise formation, where the pilots take more separation and the flight leader maneuvers more aggressively, even flying aerobatics. Four-aircraft, or division, formation is introduced and the students learn how to maintain position and maneuver in the larger groups. By the time the formation syllabus is complete, the T-45 students will have flown nearly twenty-five sorties, five of them solo and four of them at night. Nearly every subsequent flight in the remainder of the curriculum—including the weapons, air-to-air, and carrier qualification phases—will involve formation flight of some sort or another. The flying that the aviator does when he reaches the fleet will be much the same.

The weapons stage is where T-45 students are introduced to air-to-ground ordnance. This is the students' reason for being; in the fleet their job will be to kill the enemy. The FTI addresses this aspect:

Military aircraft are designed to destroy an enemy's potential to wage war. The primary means to accomplish this mission is by delivering various types of ordnance on enemy personnel, equipment, and installations. Accurate delivery of ordnance on surface targets is one of the primary missions of naval aviation and is accomplished with a wide variety of special and conventional

In the landing configuration the students fly at a specific "angle of attack," or attitude.

weapons. Delivery techniques vary as widely as the weapons themselves, and vary from conventional dives of all angles to computer-integrated loft maneuvers. To be a true professional, you—the naval aviator—must be thoroughly versed in air-to-ground delivery.

Before T-45 students are let loose with an aircraft loaded with weapons (albeit the nonexplosive, practice type), they receive quite a bit of classroom and computer-aided instruction on air-to-ground ordnance delivery. This instruction is augmented by multiple simulator sessions so that the students can become familiar with the dynamics of the weapons delivery pattern. They are taught about the ordnance-related systems aboard the aircraft and what roles they play during an air-to-ground mission. The most obvious device—the one directly in front of the student's face—is the heads-up display (HUD). It shows adjustable illuminated rings with a center dot, or "pipper," that is used for aiming the weapon. The mil setting of the pipper is changed according to the type of weapon employed and the sort of delivery parameters used. While the T-45 has a more advanced, computer-assisted bombing mode, and fleet aircraft have systems of even greater

capability, the basics of manual bombing are stressed in the training command.

Then there the basic theories of free-fall ballistics. The pupils are educated about the many different factors that can affect accuracy. First, the mil setting, or depression angle, for the pipper must be appropriately set for the weapon and delivery technique used. The pilots must fly so as to put the pipper over the target at the exact instant they reach a given point in the sky. Their aircraft must be in wings-level flight, perfectly trimmed, and at a precisely computed airspeed, dive angle, and altitude, and the pilot must apply a factor to correct for wind.

Failure to release the ordnance (e.g., bomb) inside parameters will cause it to go wide of the mark. For instance, a bomb dropped from too high will go long of the target; one that is dropped from too low will fall short. If an aircraft is in an angle of bank, or is skidding, it will

This T-45 is "dirtied up," or configured for an arrested landing. *USN/Ryan O'Connor*

U.S. Navy and Marine Corps operations are becoming more and more expeditionary and flyers must learn to take advantage of the facilities at hand. Here, an instructor briefs his students from an ad hoc setup.

Flight students, generally competitive by nature, support each other. They share information and techniques and form friendships that can last a lifetime.

An instructor briefs a strike flight. There are a lot of moving pieces that go into putting together a weapons training sortie.

A view of the rear cockpit's instrument panel during an actual flight. Notice that the standby altitude gyro is out of sync with the primary gyro.

With one T-45 safely airborne the deck crew looks to get another on its way. *USN/Dwain Willis*

errors of one student will cause the pattern to bunch up or get strung out. Poorly flown, the pattern has the potential to turn into a circus of orange-and-white training jets. Not only does training suffer, but the danger of midair collisions increases. Additionally, close attention must be paid to communications because each flier must make particular radio calls at specific times.

Then there are the actual bombing runs. A single run on the target is made each time a student makes a circuit around the pattern. The dive angles taught are ten, twenty, and thirty degrees. Approaching the appropriate point, the student must give careful consideration to rolling in from the proper distance in order to establish the correct dive angle. Turning and diving on the target requires the aircraft to be rolled until it is almost inverted, and it is not unusual for students to become disoriented on their first few runs. Power settings are also important, as is the aircrafts' trim. Once established in their dives the students are preoccupied with locating the target in their HUD; properly placing the pipper; scanning the airspeed, altitude, and dive angle; and then finally arming the aircraft and pressing the bomb release, or "pickle" button. Simply surviving the first few runs without running into the ground gives the SNAs some small feeling of success.

also cause the bomb to go off the target. Releasing it too fast will cause it to go long, while an airspeed that is too slow will cause the bomb to fall short. A steep dive angle sends the bomb long, and a shallow one drops it short. Different combinations of these mistakes can make the students' heads spin.

Reaching these perfect parameters at exactly the precise moment is obviously a very difficult task, but one for which the students have been prepared. The level of comfort and awareness with the aircraft that was built during the familiarization stage, and the visual scan developed during the various instrument stages contribute to the flyers' effectiveness in the bombing pattern. Additionally, the formation skills they recently honed are invaluable in getting all squadron members to and from the target safely.

Typically, students are often frustrated when they fly their first bombing sortie, a closely choreographed drill comprising four aircraft flying a nominally circular pattern around the target. It must be strictly flown, otherwise the

The red light reflecting just above the nose gear of this T-45 shows that the student is flying faster than he should be. An amber light would indicate that the aircraft is "on speed," while a green light would indicate a speed that is too slow. *USN/Ryan O'Connor*

The ordnance most commonly used is the Mk-76 practice bomb. Used throughout the fleet by all types of aircraft, it is a twenty-five-pound inert bomb with a smoke charge that allows the pilots to mark their hits. When available, 2.75-inch rockets can be used, and the strafing pattern is sometimes practiced even though the T-45 has no gun.

In the latter portion of this stage of T-45 training, the student is allowed to practice with the aircraft's continuously computed impact point mode. This mode is like that used by many modern aircraft systems and displays a cross on the HUD that shows where the bomb will hit if released at that instant. Rather than the pilots' having to establish and maintain a perfect set of release parameters, the aircraft onboard systems figure out the bombing solution and free the pilots to watch for enemy fire or other targets. In all, the students fly fifteen weapons sorties—several of them solo. The training received here is the underpinning for the employment of more advanced tactics and weapons systems in the fleet.

Operational navigation trains the students to fly at low level to a target using rudimentary dead-reckoning techniques. Just as their peers do in helicopter and multi-engine training, jet students learn how to plot a route and navigate from charts using only their heading indicator, airspeed indicator, and clock. They also learn how to recognize and interpret various terrain features and how to avoid obstacles, as well as how to adjust airspeed and heading to correct for deviations from a plotted course. Their peers do this training at slower airspeeds, but T-45 students plan their routes for 360 knots—more than 400 miles per hour. Getting lost at high speed is quite problematic, and students endeavor to do well enough that they never have to put their course recovery skills to use.

Being able to precisely taxi an aircraft may not seem to be too important—until one gets aboard the deck of the ship! *USN/Craig Spiering*

The Blue Angels practice formation flying more advanced than that taught during flight training. *USN/Dawn Morrison*

"The Blues"

The Blue Angels, the U.S. Navy's flight demonstration squadron, was formed on the orders of Admiral Chester Nimitz immediately after World War II and gave its first performance in 1946 flying the F6F Hellcat. Since then it has developed into what is regarded as one of the best—if not the best—military precision flying teams in the world. Its primary mission is to enhance U.S. Navy and Marine Corps recruiting while representing naval aviation as a goodwill ambassador to the American public and to governments and citizens of foreign nations. The squadron's members are to be ready for combat operations (for example, the Blue Angels formed the nucleus of VF-191 during the Korean Conflict).

In their history the "Blues" have flown nine different types of aircraft (including three versions of the F9F Panther) in front of nearly half a billion spectators. Today, the squadron operates the F/A-18, typically flying six aircraft in a show—a core of four with two solos. The team normally has at least one Marine Corps pilot, and the squadron's logistical transport is provided by "Fat Albert," a KC-130 with a Marine crew. The unit is based at NAS Pensacola, Florida, although it winters at NAF El Centro, California, to take advantage of the fine desert winter weather.

A student taxis a T-45 past a lineup of Blue Angels aircraft at NAF El Centro, the winter home of "The Blues."

The air-to-air combat phase is one of the chief culminating points of the T-45 curriculum. It begins with instruction that teaches the students how to maneuver a section (i.e., two jets) tactically. The typical arrangement puts the two aircraft in line abreast and separated by approximately a mile. Flying in this formation in a timely

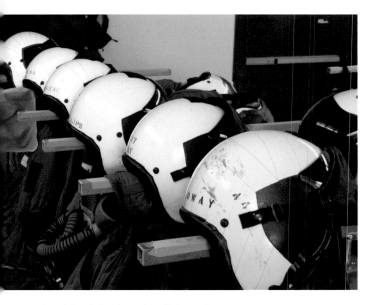

A rack loaded with student flight equipment.

and precise manner does not come instinctively, and the students work hard to learn the basics. (It will take a great deal of training beyond what they learn during this period to master all the nuances.)

Following a good grounding in the basics of tactical formation, the students are introduced to the building blocks they will use to become proficient at air combat maneuvering. To the layperson this is better known as dogfighting. Applying the basics of geometry in a three-dimensional environment while under some degree of high-g flight is a challenge, but the instruction is good and it is not long before the young fliers learn how to do a "high yo-yo" to keep from flying out in front of an adversary, or a "low yo-yo" to close the distance across a circle between their aircraft and an opposing pilot. Perhaps most important, they learn how to manage the energy of their aircraft. Making every turn a hard one in order to take difficult and fleeting shots at an adversary may leave the student low on airspeed and "dead in the water," a sitting duck for a savvy enemy flyer. So, depending on the situation, it may be smarter to wait a little longer, press an offensive advantage, and maintain airspeed before going for a kill.

Of course the students don't get to practice being on the offensive all the time. They get plenty of opportunities

The landing signal officer is responsible for getting each aircraft safely aboard the aircraft carrier. *USN/Milosz Reterski*

The blur created by photographic technique is a good representation of the typical student's experience during his first couple of "traps."
USN/Konstandinos Goumanidis

Away he goes. The "shooter" has just given the signal to launch this T-45 from the catapult. *USN/Ryan O'Connor*

to experience the difficulty inherent in trying to neutralize an enemy that is pressing hard. The very challenging art of fighting back to a position that is at least neutral is taught, if not mastered. Sometimes it is best to recognize when a chance to disengage is presented and live to fight another day.

After some practice in developing his one-versus-one skills, individual students are paired with other SNAs, and the two work together to prosecute an "enemy" aircraft flown by an experienced instructor. This is when the tactical formation skills they learned earlier are put to use. They also learn how to take advantage of the strengths of a two-ship formation over a single aircraft. Working together, they team up—one aircraft at a time—to beat down the instructor before one of them delivers the final killing shot. Maneuvering the section through the sky and using good communications while keeping track of all the aircraft all of the time is a difficult exercise. The instructors are talented pilots, and the students get manhandled as often as they win an engagement. These flights are a good, basic introduction to the very dynamic and stressful environment of air warfare.

The final stage of the T-45 students' training varies depending on a number of factors, but the availability of a fleet aircraft carrier for carrier qualification (CQ) training is the biggest driver. It is perhaps the most challenging of all the training events in naval aviation. There is no tactical jet, Navy or Marine, that does not fly from an aircraft carrier; the ability to do so safely and effectively is an absolute requisite for naval aviators who operate tactical jets.

Since their first familiarization, or contact, flights, the T-45 students have practiced every landing as if it were taking place aboard "the boat." Absolutely precise airspeed and attitude control, as well as strict adherence to the prescribed pattern, are drilled into the new flyers from the very beginning. Even after the familiarization stage, students save fuel on nearly every sortie so that they can practice several landings to further develop the skills that will be required to bring the T-45 aboard the ship. There is even a separate training module that includes seven flights dedicated entirely to practicing carrier landings at the airfield. This module takes place earlier in the syllabus to ensure that students receive the training they will need before advancing.

Training in the second, later, module begins a couple of weeks prior to the day when the students actually take their jets to the ship. This phase begins with lectures about the ship and the proper way to operate around and on it.

The deck crew guides a student into the catapult track. *USN/Dwain Willis*

Of course, techniques are taught to help the students further refine their flying so that they stand a good chance of successfully completing the evolution. Very few people outside naval aviation understand that the students never get a chance to go to the ship with an instructor; the first time they see the aircraft carrier they are alone in the aircraft!

They are given eleven field carrier landing practice sorties. These are similar to the sorties in the first module but culminate in an event at the actual aircraft carrier. Almost all of these flights are flown solo and are wholly dedicated to the students' exacting control of their T-45s in a simulated aircraft carrier landing pattern. Each landing is extensively evaluated, graded, and critiqued by landing signal officers (LSOs). These are experienced pilots whose job it is to monitor and control the landings aboard ship; they are demanding of the students, just as they are of their fellow aviators in the fleet. Aided by a unique

The constricted confines of the cockpit. The tangle of straps and buckles that makes up the pilot's flight gear is apparent. *USMC/John Andress*

shorthand designed specifically for grading landings aboard the carrier, after each flight the LSOs debrief the students, landing by landing. Initially it is confusing, but the students quickly catch on and take advantage of its utility to improve their performance. An example might be "LIGHFOSX(SIM)BIC(TMPBAR-IW)," which translates as "long in the groove, high fast overshooting start, a slight settle in the middle, flat in close, a bit too much power and flat at the ramp to in the wires."

At the heart of the effort to get aboard the aircraft carrier is the final fifteen to twenty seconds when the pilot rolls the wings level in "the groove" and flies the aircraft to touchdown. Airspeed and angle of attack must be precisely controlled to within just a couple of knots. The lineup must be near perfect because an off-center engagement of the arresting cables can damage the aircraft or the arresting gear. And the glide slope must be strictly maintained so that the touchdown is on the exact spot of the deck that will allow the tailhook to grab one of the arresting cables.

It is the Fresnel lens optical landing system that the naval aviator uses to determine whether or not he is on the correct glideslope. Positioned on the left side of the runway or ship, the Fresnel lens is a composite of mirrored lights of different colors. Horizontally, there is a line of green datum lights. Centered in the datum lights is a vertical column of yellow lights. If the pilot is exactly on

The wingman's view. *USMC/John Andress*

glide slope, the yellow light, or "ball," in the center column will line up precisely with the horizontal green datum lights; this is known as a "centered ball." If the pilot is too high, the ball will be above the green datum lights; too low, and the ball will be below the lights. If the pilot is dangerously low, the ball will be at the bottom of the vertical column and will glow red. If the approach is too dangerous to continue, there are two rows of vertical red lights flanking each side of the central column. The LSO illuminates these "waveoff" lights to order the pilot to discontinue the approach.

Ideally, the pilot will roll wings level about three quarters of a mile astern the ship with a centered ball and will keep the ball exactly centered while maintaining a perfect airspeed, angle of attack, and lineup. A perfect trap, with the tailhook catching the number-three wire, should result. This is hardly ever the reality, though, and the typical approach to the ship finds the aviator making constant corrections to small deviations until the instant of touchdown on the deck. It is approximately seventeen seconds of the most intense flying in the aviation world.

The day students go to the ship is perhaps the most nerve-wracking of not only their aviation career but quite likely their entire life. Few are the young pilots who are able to sleep soundly the day before their "Charlie" time—that period in which they are expected to be over the aircraft carrier, prepared to land. They fly to the ship solo, usually on the wing of an instructor, and are normally quite taken aback at the sight of the "tiny" ship plying the water below them. Nevertheless, their training takes over and they react appropriately when they are directed to descend and enter the pattern for four touch and goes. The touch-and-go landings give them an opportunity to clear some butterflies from their stomachs and gain confidence before they make their first arrested landings. It is rather common for young aviators to "fly the ball" quite well all the way until close to the deck, and then become distracted by the size and novelty of the ship. Usually an LSO can refocus the students' efforts with a choice phrase or two.

Once cleared for an arrested landing, the SNAs will lower their arresting hooks and fly the aircraft just as before. If they handle the aircraft properly, they typically will be stunned at the violence of being jerked to a halt from an airspeed of more than 100 knots. It usually takes the temporarily stupefied neophytes a second or two to get their bearings before following the directions that the deck crew members are emphatically waving so that they can clear the landing area for the next aircraft.

When clear, students may be directed to take on more fuel or may be sent to the catapult for launch. The SNAs must be absolutely attentive to the different deck crews and follow their instructions without hesitation. Although they are still ultimately responsible for their aircraft, it is the deck crew that gets the pilots where they need to go, when they need to be there.

The catapult "shot" is one of the biggest thrills in aviation. The students are carefully directed into position, and their planes' launch bars are connected to a shuttle that, in turn, is attached to the steam-powered piston that ultimately accelerates the aircraft across the deck of the ship at greater than 100 knots in less than two seconds. Once the individual flyers have completed their checklists and brought the engine up to full power—and double-checked that everything is in order—they give the signal that they are ready to go with a smart salute to a yellow-shirted catapult officer. A second or so later, the officer touches the deck, and the aircraft get rocketed off the end of the ship.

It is a feeling difficult to describe. First, new pilots experience an instant of helplessness—a realization that they have absolutely zero control over what is taking place. Once the catapult stroke has begun, there is nothing that will stop it—the aircraft is going off the end of the ship. Physically, the flyers feel as if their lower guts are being lifted into the upper body. It is a ticklish, but not unpleasant sensation similar to, but more intense than, some of the more radical carnival rides. And of course, there is the g-force that holds the pilots like glue until the aircraft clears the ship and becomes airborne.

Once they are flying, and climbing away from the water, the students have little time to reflect on what just happened. In only a few seconds they turn back into the pattern to set up for another landing. In all, they will be required to complete four touch-and-go and ten arrested landings. If they execute them to the satisfaction of the LSO, they will be considered "quals" and will have completed one of the most demanding evolutions in aviation.

Students who complete the tactical strike syllabus in the T-45, will have flown more than 160 hours in the aircraft as well as more than 100 hours in the simulator. The longest and most comprehensive of the Navy's flight-training syllabi, the course will have taken approximately one year.

Stretching more than 1,000 feet long with a flight deck that covers 4.5 acres, the USS *George Washington* is a key instrument of our nation's diplomacy. *USN*

EIGHT

An AV-8B Harrier pilot conducting post-start checks. *USN/Anibal Rivera*

The Fleet

A deck handler directs an aircraft while an F/A-18F Super Hornet prepares to slam down behind him. *USN/Chad McNeeley*

The day finally comes when the students who possess the talent, perseverance, motivation, and—to some degree—luck, finally fly their last training-command sortie. Regardless of the syllabus, they are often met on the flight line by fellow students, instructors, and sometimes family, for a congratulatory dousing. This is also where they are sometimes awarded their "soft wings"—a leather nametag embossed with the coveted Wings of Gold. On the spot, their student nametag is unceremoniously peeled away from its Velcro backing and replaced with the new one. Depending on the pipeline through which they passed, and the efficiency of the training command during that period, the

Life as a naval aviator is never far from death. *USN/Andrea Decanini*

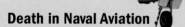

Death in Naval Aviation

It is a romantic profession. And part of the romance is associated with the danger that is part and parcel of naval aviation. It is a danger that costs lives.

Not so long ago the U.S. Navy and Marine Corps lost hundreds of aircraft each year along with many of the pilots and crews who flew them. Death in naval aviation was a daily occurrence during the 1950s; the Navy and the Corps crashed an average of two aircraft a day. Dramatic improvements in aviation safety have decreased the accident rate to the point that a single aircraft is lost about every ten days or so; some even argue that there is little that can be done to reduce the rate further. Still, death happens often enough that everyone who makes a career of naval aviation will sooner or later lose a friend.

effort took anywhere from just more than a year, to well more than two. Along the way about one in five students who started the program at API have been washed out.

Soft-winging aside, the real excitement occurs in a more formal setting. Navy pilots count many important events in their lives, including their wedding days and the births of their children. Probably the most important date after those is the day they are formally designated a naval aviator. The ceremony usually includes anywhere from a handful to a dozen or more students and is typically held at the base club, presided over by the air wing commodore. Friends and family from all over the country converge to witness the proceedings. Usually, the commodore recognizes the individuals one at a time and presents the wings to a member of the student's family—often the wife or mother—who then pins them above the graduates' left breast. It is a remarkable achievement and an emotional moment, not only for the newly fledged aviator but also for the very proud family. (The celebration following the event often becomes raucous.)

The new aviators have usually received orders assigning them to particular aircraft by the time they have been "winged," or designated. The orders are based first on the needs of the different services and second on the desires

Sailors bow their heads during services for a lost aviator. *USN/Michael Damron*

150

of the individual pilots and their performance record. Typically, aviators with the highest grades during the period they were designated receive their first choice. The playing field is wide open after that, and the other designated aviators of a given group are at the mercy of their branch of service.

The choices are narrowing. Twenty years ago, Navy and Marine jet students could have been assigned to any one of seven different aircraft. Today, Navy jet students can expect orders to only one of the versions of the F/A-18, or the EA-6B. Marine Corps jet students can expect orders to the F/A-18, the AV-8B, or the EA-6B. On the other hand, the choices for the maritime multi-engine aircraft students have not changed at all. And of course, neither has the E-2C or C-2A assignment changed. The choices for Navy rotary-wing assignments have narrowed, with the SH-60 as the most numerous variant. Marine Corps rotary-wing assignments have remained unchanged, except that the possibility exists that students can be slated for the new MV-22 Osprey.

The obligation to serve, or "payback," that comes with flight training often changes in terms and conditions, and sometimes varies from service to service. Currently, the requirement is that officers must stay on active duty for six additional years after being designated a naval aviator if they receive orders to fly helicopters or turboprop-powered

A missing-man formation scythes overhead at the conclusion of a memorial service for a lost pilot. *USN/Jay Pugh*

The sparks are caused by the metal hook of this E-2C scraping the metal flight deck. *USN/Mark Rebilas*

Low over the sands of Iraq, an armed U.S. Marine UH-1N throws up dirt and debris. *USMC/Samuel Bard Valliere*

aircraft. Those assigned to jets incur an eight-year obligation after receiving their wings.

As much as they would like it to be different, the new naval aviators are not quite finished being students. In order to learn to fly their assigned aircraft, they are sent to an FRS, or fleet replacement squadron. These are special units that have the mission of training pilots to operate a particular aircraft. There are currently more than twenty Marine and Navy FRSs concentrated mainly along both coasts, but that number will decrease as the Navy finishes phasing out different airframes such as the F-14 and the S-3, and consolidates training for other types.

Depending on the aircraft, students may be in the FRS for anywhere from several months to more than a year before being assigned to their first fleet unit. This is where the nation will start to reap a return on the huge investment it has made to create the new naval aviator. Youngsters are

An interesting perspective of an SH-60 Seahawk. *USN/Milosz Reterski*

Left: One of the S-3's primary roles during the past few years has been aerial refueling of other aircraft. *USN/Alex Witte*

not given the most complex missions or tasks when they arrive, but they are expected to be proficient flyers, and they continue to learn by flying operationally. As they gain experience they are given more and more responsibility. Indeed, recent actions have seen newcomers assigned straight to combat over Iraq.

After arriving at their first squadron, the new pilots are given jobs that are not directly related to flying, but are nonetheless essential to the operation of the unit. For instance a new officer might be assigned to work in the administrative or legal section, or in logistics. It is also common for pilots to work in the various offices that perform maintenance on the aircraft. Nearly all these jobs will require them to learn to lead sailors or Marines and to help them in meeting their mission; they must learn quickly because they are held accountable for the success or failure of their men and women. Fortunately, all the

Skippering an aircraft carrier is one of the most demanding and rewarding jobs in naval aviation. Here the captain of the *Harry S Truman* watches replenishment operations while the ship is under way. Note the SH-60 in the background moving material from ship to ship. *USN/Mark Gleason*

The U.S. Navy has few MH-53E helicopters remaining in service. *USN/Christopher Mobley*

Because the aircraft does not need to rearm to execute its mission, the EA-6B can stay airborne for nearly as long as its crews can stay awake—fuel permitting. *USN/Erik Gudmundson (USAF)*

Commanding an Aircraft Carrier

The path that leads to the command of an aircraft carrier must include designation as a naval aviator or naval flight officer. In other words, only an aviator can command one of these complicated floating airbases. However, it takes more than flying savvy to be assigned to skipper an aircraft carrier. Those who gain command of these big ships have shown that they have the requisite intelligence, leadership ability, and tactical acumen. They will have already shown these attributes through their entire career and successfully commanded at the squadron level.

They will also have served in enough staff billets to ensure that they have mastered not only the war-fighting side of their art but the strategic and political aspects, as well. Those being groomed to take the reins of an aircraft carrier must pass through the U.S. Navy's Nuclear Power School. And they must successfully command a different type of deep-draft ship (usually a large support or amphibious vessel).

Generally, it is tactical jet aviators who understandably get command of the aircraft carriers, although it is not unheard of for an E-2C officer or a helicopter pilot to be slated for the position. An inordinate number of Naval Academy graduates seem to be awarded with the commands, but it must be remembered that the academy produces almost 40 percent of the service's aviators.

The ceremony that marks the student's designation as a naval aviator is called a "winging." *USN/Tom Thomas*

services are staffed with experienced cadres of noncommissioned officers capable of helping the new officers learn their roles.

There is no single description that covers all the different lifestyles or types of flying in naval aviation. Tactical jet pilots feel that they spend most of their lives aboard the aircraft carrier or deployed overseas. Helicopter crews argue that they spend just as much time at sea. The flyers of the big P-3Cs and C-130s do not go afloat, but they also spend much time away from home. It takes a special sort of marriage and family to withstand the stress of constant separation and the danger that are part of everyday life for naval aviators. Recent operations in Iraq and elsewhere around the world have driven the operations tempo as high as it has ever been.

A typical first tour in a fleet squadron lasts anywhere from two to four years. The possible assignments following this initial period are quite varied but are usually not flying jobs (in the U.S. Navy these stints are called disassociated tours). The flyers who are now seasoned may go to serve on a staff anywhere in the country or across the globe. It is also common to return to the training command as an instructor, or to be assigned to recruiting duty. Marine Corps pilots often take an assignment as a forward air controller (FAC), also known as a joint terminal attack controller (JTAC). Professional schools, too, draw a substantial number of officers.

Subsequent squadron tours see the pilots taking jobs in the unit that demand more work and responsibility. Flying becomes almost a secondary duty, while the actual operation of the squadron requires the lion's share of their energy. The most demanding of these department-head billets are the operations officer and maintenance officer assignments. Their performance in these jobs—in some combination with their flying skills—will largely determine their suitability for command.

After their second flying tour, pilots can expect more of the same types of nonflying assignments they had earlier in their careers but at a higher level and with more responsibility. Duty in the Pentagon will draw more of them than previously, as will service on various fleet staffs. There are fewer flight instructor billets, and assignments to the field are fewer for the Marine Corps officers. Professional schools take on more importance, and those who are interested in making the service a lifetime career take more care to pad their resumes with more meaningful assignments.

Not everyone can stay in the service to become an admiral or a general. There comes a time, usually after about ten years of service or so, when a significant number of officers start to separate from the U.S. Navy, Marine Corps, and Coast Guard. The reasons are many and include a desire to spend more time with family, the pursuit of other careers or interests, or often simply a weariness of the naval aviation lifestyle. Regardless, after having faithfully served in one of the most dangerous jobs in the world, there is no stigma attached to leaving. Indeed, these men and women go with the gratitude of their nation and with the friendship and best wishes of the comrades they leave behind. They carry with them the skills they learned as pilots, and perhaps the more useful skills they learned as officers and leaders. They have the satisfaction of knowing that they attempted and mastered one of the most demanding and rewarding careers the world can offer. They will always be able to look on their Wings of Gold with pride.

This is how most nonflyers may expect to experience a catapult launch; C-2A Greyhounds take personnel from ship to shore. Unlike the pilots, passengers face backward. *USN/Craig Spiering*

It is ironic that near the end of its service life the F-14 Tomcat really became useful as a bomber. *USN/Mark Rebilas*

Index

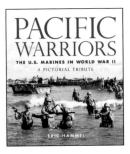

Pacific Warriors
ISBN 0-7603-2097-7

Hunting al Qaeda
ISBN 0-7603-2252-x

The Blue Angels
ISBN 0-7603-2216-3

Other books in the To Be A . . . Series:

To Be a U.S. Army Ranger
ISBN 0-7603-1314-8

To Be a U.S. Navy SEAL
ISBN 0-7603-1404-7

To Be a U.S. Air Force Pilot
ISBN 0-7603-1791-7

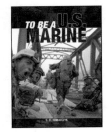

To Be a U.S. Marine
ISBN 0-7603-1788-7

To Be an FBI Special Agent
ISBN 0-7603-2118-3

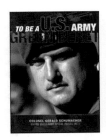

To Be a U.S. Army Green Beret
ISBN 0-7603-2107-8